The Saint Play
In Medieval Europe

Early Drama, Art, and Music
Monograph Series, 8

A new Enterlude, neuer

before this tyme imprinted, entreating of the
Life and Repentaunce of Marie Magdalene : not only
godlie, learned and fruitefull, but also well furnished with plea-
saunt myrth and pastime, very delectable for those
which shall heare or reade the same.
Made by the learned clarke
Lewis Wager.

The names of the Players.

Infidelitie the Uice.
Marie Magdalene.
Pride of life.
Cupiditie.
Carnall Concupiscence.
Simon the Pharisie.
Malicious Iudgement.

The Lawe.
Knowledge of sinne.
Christ Iesus.
Fayth.
Repentaunce.
Iustification.
Loue.

Foure may easely play this Enterlude.

Imprinted at London, by Iohn Charlewood,
dwelling in Barbican, at the signe of the halfe Eagle
and the Key. Anno. 1567.

Title page of the *Life and Repentaunce of Marie Magdalene* (1567). Courtesy of the British Library.

The Saint Play
in Medieval Europe

Edited by
Clifford Davidson

papers by
Clyde W. Brockett, Clifford Davidson, Lynette R. Muir,
Kathleen C. Falvey, Peter Happé, and John Wasson

Early Drama, Art, and Music
Monograph Series, 8

MEDIEVAL INSTITUTE PUBLICATIONS
Western Michigan University
Kalamazoo, Michigan
1986

ISBN: 0-918720-77-x
ISBN: 0-918720-78-8 (paperback)

Printed in the United States of America

CONTENTS

LIST OF ILLUSTRATIONS

Frontispiece. Title page of the *Life and Repentaunce of Marie Magdalene* (1567).

Plates:

1. The Jew praying to St. Nicholas. Painted glass, St. Severus Chapel, Rouen Cathedral.

2. St. Denys. Painted glass, Church of St. Denys, York.

3. The Martyrdom of St. Denys and St. Denys carrying his head before a church. Cloister boss, Norwich Cathedral.

4. The Martyrdom of St. Denys. Manuscript illumination by the Master of the Queen Mary Psalter. Bodleian Library MS. Canon Misc. 248, fol. 45^v (detail).

5. The Martyrdom of St. Lawrence. Painted glass, York Minster nave.

6. Seraph appearing to St. Francis. Manuscript illumination by Matthew Paris. Corpus Christi College MS. 16, fol. 66^v.

7. Life of St. Catherine. Wall Painting, Sporle, Norfolk.

8. St. Catherine refuses to worship idol. Alabaster. British Museum.

9. The Martyrdom of St. Thomas Becket. Alabaster. British Museum.

10. St. George receives armor from the Blessed Virgin Mary. Restored painted glass, St. Neot, Cornwall.

11. St. Mary Magdalene. Painted screen (detail), Wiggenhall.

12. Lucas van Leyden, *The Worldly Pleasures of Mary Magdalene*. Engraving.

13. Hortulanus scene, with Mary Magdalene and Risen Christ. Roof boss, nave, Norwich Cathedral.

14. Mary Magdalene. Detail from painted glass, East Harling, Norfolk.

15. St. Barbe defeats the pagan doctors in argument. Painted roof, Church of St Martin-des-Connées.

16. St. Barbe defies her Mother, the Queen. Painted roof, Church of St Martin-des-Connées.

17. St. George triumphs over the magician Athanaise whose poisoned cup has killed the man at saint's feet though the saint himself is unharmed. Woodcarving, choir stalls, St. George's Chapel, Windsor Castle.

18. St. Herculaneum holding image with structures around Great Square in Perugia, structures now altered or destroyed. Painted by Meo di Guido or his collaborator. National Gallery, Perugia.

19. Beheading of St. John the Baptist. Painted by Giannicola di Paolo, 1515. Chapel of St. John the Baptist, Collegio del Cambio, Perugia.

Preface

The saint play of the Middle Ages is a neglected genre which has not received the scholarly attention it has deserved. Hence the present book, which is an attempt at a collaborative survey, aims to provide a much needed introduction to what may well have been the most popular type of drama in the medieval period. In keeping with the aims of the Early Drama, Art, and Music project and its publication series, the emphasis here tends to be on cross-disciplinary study rather than merely literary analysis. Each contributor to the volume was assigned a specific area, with major emphasis being placed on the saint play in England while there was also a determination not to neglect the manifestations of the genre on the continent. In the best of all possible worlds it would have been desirable to have included specific articles focusing on some further language areas, especially Cornish, German, Dutch, and Spanish; however, some of the plays in these languages are nevertheless given limited treatment in this volume.

In preparing the studies which are included here, the authors have all been heavily indebted to previous scholars who have opened up many of the questions which are given attention here. More specifically, we are grateful to all those, including librarians at our own institutions and at libraries in the countries being surveyed, who have aided our work in various ways. We have also passed drafts of our essays around among ourselves—a source of most valuable suggestions that have benefited all of us. Additional comments came to us from those who attended the sessions on the saint play at the International Congress on Medieval Studies two years ago, and to them we are most grateful.

My own gratitude is extended to my collaborators in

ix

PREFACE

this volume for their cooperation throughout the time when
this book was in the making. Their conscientiousness at every
phase in the preparation of the book made the editing task
a joy. I should also like to thank Medieval Institute Publications, especially Juleen Eichinger and Thomas Seiler, for
their tolerance and their kindnesses during the seeing of this
book through the press.

Clifford Davidson

Introduction

Clifford Davidson

If, as John Wasson has suggested, that type of medieval drama which focuses on the life and/or martyrdom of a saint is to be detected in the background of Renaissance tragedy,[1] the saint play in addition to its intrinsic value may be said to function as a link in the development of one of the most admired dramatic forms in the history of the theater in the West. Such a theory concerning the relationship between medieval and Renaissance drama may, to be sure, be unfashionable as yet, since brilliant work by O. B. Hardison, Jr., has demonstrated the faultiness of the evolutionary model of development when applied to the history of early drama.[2] Nevertheless, the historical dimension, set apart from preconceptions about the *evolution* of forms—i.e., evolution especially as a principle resembling the biological model associated with Darwin—needs careful examination, and indeed it is not possible to understand cultural phenomena such as the drama or theater without attention to the establishment of traditions, expectations, common practices, and attitudes. The saint play, either in its Latin musical form or in its mainly spoken vernacular forms, does not exist apart from the cultic practices which nourished it, and neither does the drama of the Renaissance stand entirely apart from the conventions and expectations of the medieval stage, including its habit of responding to sensational theatrical effects in the conclusions of the plays on the lives and martyrdoms of the saints. While we must with Hardison strongly reject the notion of the survival of the fittest and the idea of evolution from lower to higher forms in the history of Western drama

1

to the time of Shakespeare, there is every reason to examine the historical evidence for the genre of the European saint play, its origins in the practices of the Church, its role in civic culture, and its transformations in the Reformation and Renaissance.

The cult of the saints in the West developed at an early date, as the *Martyrdom of St. Polycarp* indicates. This second-century document describes how this saint's followers reacted after his martyrdom on 23 February 155 (or 156) A.D.:

> taking up his bones, more precious than the richest jewels, and tried above gold, [we] deposited them where it was fitting: where, being gathered together as we have opportunity, with joy and gladness, the Lord shall grant unto us to celebrate the anniversary of his martyrdom, both in memory of those who have suffered, and for the exercise and preparation of those that may hereafter suffer.[3]

Already the collecting of relics and the identifying of the anniversary of the death of the martyr as a festival day are recognized as practices of the Church. Only later, beginning with St. Martin of Tours,[4] were *confessors* recognized along with martyrs as saints whose entry into the eternal kingdom could also benefit those in this world who had not yet entered that kingdom.

The veneration of the saints, often at first associated with churches such as those built up around the periphery of Rome or other cities (e.g., Perugia, which is discussed by Kathleen Falvey in her article on the Perugian saint play in this volume), thus early became an important aspect of medieval Christianity. As Peter Brown has noted, the saints provided a connection very like a kinship relationship between the individual believer and the community of believers;[5] through the experience of access to the saint, the worshipper was further able to experience the state which Victor Turner has called "liminality."[6] In the veneration of the saint, the person separates himself or herself from the society and the normal experiences of everyday life, partic-

2

ipates with others in a communal and transcendental ritual, and then returns to everyday life as one who has been enriched and changed.[7] Such experiences were most intense as the worshippers took part in pilgrimages (e.g., those which after 1170 would be directed to the famous shrine of St. Thomas Becket at Canterbury) or as people formed congregations at the vigil of the saint or at the services of the saint's day. Indeed, the veneration of saints became deeply imbedded in the liturgy, as any cursory look at, for example, the Sarum Breviary will demonstrate.[8] Also, E. Catherine Dunn has forcefully reminded us that the reciting of saints' legends was even more important in the earlier Gallican liturgy, and this recitation, joined perhaps with liturgical acts such as processions with relics, may have played a role in the development of drama in the medieval Church.[9]

There is, however, another dimension that is of the greatest importance if we are to understand the phenomenology of the saints, and that is the *visual aspect*. First of all, the person devoted to the veneration of the saint—a person who may well be hoping for personal benefit from contact with the holiness of the saint—would desire to achieve as much closeness as possible to the saint. Such closeness could be achieved through being in proximity to relics, which as we know were very widely disseminated in the medieval period; further, certain relics, more highly valued than others, thus provided the motive for pilgrimage. Closeness to the saint could be achieved, however, by another means—by contemplation of the devotional image of the saint. As Richard C. Trexler and others have demonstrated, the line of demarcation between the image—i.e., the visual representation—and the prototype is very blurred in actual medieval practice; the image could be treated as if it had sensory awareness, and it evidenced "psychic power."[10] The *visual experience* of the saint therefore is regarded as a valuable thing. Finally, it should be noted that "visual experience" of a saint could also be achieved by means of representation of scenes from his or her life and martyrdom in medieval drama. The wonder is that the so-called liturgical drama—the music-drama of the Middle Ages—did not earlier take up subjects associated with the saints of both the biblical and post-biblical periods.

Biblical saints do, of course, figure in such later music-dramas as the Benediktbeuern Passion Play with its famous presentation of Mary Magdalene as a prostitute purchasing cosmetics to make herself more attractive to men prior to her conversion in addition to the presence in this play of a Lazarus scene. There is also the full-length *Raising of Lazarus* found in the twelfth-century Fleury Playbook, as well as a play on the same subject by Hilarius.[11] As biblical saints, the two disciples in the *Peregrinus* are further examples that, in addition to St. Thomas who appears in the play, help to provide visual access to the mystery of the redemption of the race by the Christian Savior.[12] The earliest music-dramas or dramatic ceremonies, however, had focused only on such figures as the holy women at the tomb of Christ on the first Easter, to which were added an extended scene with Mary Magdalene and two apostles.[13]

On the other hand, St. Paul, who appears in the New Testament initially under the name of Saul as a persecutor of Christians, provides rich material from which to choose episodes for dramatization, but it is the most famous of these scenes, his conversion, that is treated in another of the dramas in the Fleury Playbook.[14] This drama stages Saul's campaign (here assisted by two armed knights) against Christians, his zealous setting forth to Damascus, and his encounter with Jesus on the road to that city as well as his continuation of the journey in a blinded state, his reception in Damascus, his receipt of guidance from Ananias, and his preaching, which causes hostility to break out against him. Finally, the play concludes with his flight back to Jerusalem, where he is introduced to the other disciples by Barnabas. The ending is marked by the singing of *Te Deum laudamus*.[15] As Karl Young notes, this play could logically have been performed "only on the feast of the Conversion of St. Paul, January 25th," probably at Matins.[16]

Fortunately, the rubrics to the play text also include

4

some extensive stage directions, which indicate that a platform on the one side is to represent Jerusalem while the
playing area on the other side will be identified as Damascus.
Details, such as Ananias reclining on a bed and Paul lowered
"as if from the walls" of Damascus, tend to support a picture
of a theatrical event separated quite clearly from ritual or
ceremony.

The various scenes of the drama are also the ones prominent in the Conversion of St. Paul cycles of illustrations in
contemporary bibles—cycles which owe much to traditions
of narrative illustration that originated in Carolingian times.[17]
Thus Saul's receipt of letters from the High Priest in Jerusalem is depicted in a historiated initial in a Bible in the
Vatican Library;[18] in the manuscript illustration, the priest,
wearing the typical Jewish hat, is seated at the left as he
hands the letter to Saul. In a manuscript from the Municipal
Library at Avranches, Saul's companions are in armor, while
in front of them he has fallen to the ground and out of a
cloud the hand of God is reaching down with rays, presumably representing lightning, extending from his fingers.[19] As
in the music-drama, Saul is a pedestrian, and too when he
falls he is not prostrate. The Avranches Bible also shows him
having been taken to Damascus by two men, at least one of
them in armor (the other is hidden behind the first).[20] Further illuminations in contemporary bibles show Ananias
healing the saint and feeding him, followed by the baptism
of the saint, his preaching in Damascus, and his escape from
the city.[21] The play only omits the baptism scene, though it
adds St. Paul's acceptance as an apostle in Jerusalem.

The music-dramas of St. Nicholas—the subject of the
paper in this volume by Clyde W. Brockett, who provides
analysis of those examples with musical notation—comprise
a full saint play cycle in the Fleury Playbook, and there are
also further examples of Latin plays on this saint without
extant music.[22] The survival of these plays may well have
much to do with the popularity of the saint and his feast day
as well as with the presence of his relics. As the article by
Professor Brockett points out, there may have been a direct

connection between the cult of St. Nicholas, a papal visit to France, and, not impossibly, the drama. In any case, the Fleury plays representing aspects of the legend of St. Nicholas make up the earliest extant music-dramas which can also be classified as post-biblical saint plays.

For the vernacular saint play in Europe, however, we have examples which dramatize the lives of a great many saints—plays with regional characeristics of the greatest significance and with widely differing iconographic details— from across the continent as well as from the British Isles. Articles included in this book discuss the English, French, and Italian examples, but records and/or texts of such drama also are present for other European language areas.[23] Among the plays from Britain, there is even a Cornish example, *Beunans Meriasek*, of considerable interest for what it teaches us about staging and about the theatrical presentation of legendary material.[24] Written c.1475-1500, this drama is based on the legend of the Breton saint, Meriasek or Meriadocus, the patron saint of Camborne, Cornwall. At his death, which to be sure is not caused by martyrdom, he indicates (ll. 4293-97) that he will be venerated at the parish church founded by him and dedicated to him near the church of St. Mary in Camborne "even though my body lie elsewhere."[25] His feast day in early June (marked as the first Friday in this month at Camborne until the eighteenth century[26]) would have been an appropriate date for the play, which apparently was presented out of doors over a three-day period, presumably concluding on Sunday. The manuscript of the play, copied by a scribe named Ralph Ton in 1504,[27] contains two drawings showing stage plans; these are attached to the first two parts of the play.[28] *Beunans Meriasek* was staged in the round, with hell to the North and heaven to the East (i.e., at the top of the diagram); in the center of the playing area on Day I was a chapel, while on the second day there was a change at this spot to a representation of St. Samson's Church at Dol, Brittany.

Being far less dependent on the liturgy than the music-dramas, the vernacular plays are therefore more closely aligned with iconographic traditions of the time. Hence it is possible to provide evidence concerning the probable content of certain dramas for which we have only notices in dramatic records but no texts or other direct evidence concerning them. A number of such lost plays from England are discussed in my extended article on "The Middle English Saint Play and Its Iconography," below.

Most frequently the vernacular plays were civic productions, gathering together townsmen or citizens and performers (e.g., minstrels) to stage dramas that would bring honor on the town or city at the same time that they might provide an opportunity for imaginative and devotional experiences among their audiences. The scenes that were presented on the vernacular stage were also certainly characterized by a less stylized manner of playing than in the case of the Latin dramas. We can expect too that such aspects as costume were more consistent with iconographic traditions than with liturgical practice. Evidence for the elaborateness of such saint plays is contained in such documents as a property list for a St. George play possibly performed at Turin in 1429.[29] Nevertheless, like the work of the Flemish painters, any apparent tendency toward "realism" was balanced by a thorough use of symbolism and iconographically determined detail. Hence a St. Christopher play at Valencia gives the saint "a blue tunic to be worn underneath" and presumably over it another with "fish painted on it"[30]—a detail which attempts to reproduce the fish normally included in representations of Christopher in the visual arts.

In much of Northern Europe, however, the Reformation spelled the end of the older Catholic saint play with its emphasis on devotion and on the cult of the saints, often coordinated with local practices of veneration. In England, where iconoclasm was more severe than, for example, in Lutheran countries,[31] an active propagandist like John Bale could nevertheless use the theater to argue for a thoroughly revised understanding of sainthood. The vigor of Bale's work, its dependence on older dramatic forms, and its tendency to break with past iconographic traditions are discussed in the

7

article in this book by Peter Happé, who also extends his treatment to other dramas of this period.

It may, of course, be claimed that the saint play is a perennial form, emerging again in various transformations up to the present time. In our century, the medieval form has been popularized by such a writer as T. S. Eliot, whose *Murder in the Cathedral* focuses on the martyrdom of St. Thomas Becket, a saint who had become a particularly admired example of heroism to those of Eliot's ecclesiastical persuasion.[32] But the focus of the studies in this book must be on the period prior to the middle of the seventeenth century and especially on the examples from the medieval period. If the medieval saint play establishes significant traditions of staging and dramatic structure which were passed on to later historical periods, as Professor Wasson believes, the examination of plays in the corpus of early drama also serves a useful purpose in helping us to come to terms with the theatrical dimension of the cult of the saints in medieval religion. But, as the extant texts of such plays from the Middle Ages have demonstrated in recent years, these can be very good dramas for the stage—lively, complex, and theatrically effective.

NOTES

[1]John Wasson, "The Morality Play: Ancestor of Elizabethan Drama," *Comparative Drama*, 13 (1979), 215-20; rpt. in *Drama in the Middle Ages*, ed. Clifford Davidson, C. J. Gianakaris, and John H. Stroupe (New York: AMS Press, 1982), pp. 321-26, and see also the same author's article "The Secular Saint Plays of the Elizabethan Era," below.

[2]See Hardison's chapter entitled "Darwin, Mutations, and the Origin of Medieval Drama," *Christian Rite and Christian Drama in the Middle Ages* (Baltimore: Johns Hopkins Press, 1965), pp. 1-34.

[3]Translation in *The Apostolic Fathers*, introd. Dr. Burton (London: Griffith, Farran, Okeden, and Welsh, n.d.), II, 164.

[4]Josef A. Jungmann, *The Early Liturgy to the Time of Gregory the Great*, trans. Francis A. Brunner (1959; rpt. London: Darton, Longman, and Todd, n.d.), p. 181.

[5]Peter Brown, *The Cult of the Saints* (Chicago: Univ. of Chicago Press, 1981), p. 31.

[6]See especially Victor Turner and Edith Turner, *Image and Pilgrimage in Christian Culture* (New York: Columbia Univ. Press, 1978), pp. 1-39.

[7]See also Brown, *Cult of the Saints*, p. 42.

[8]See the typical Sarum Breviary printed at Paris by C. Chevallon and F. Regnault in 1531 [STC 1530].

[9]See E. Catherine Dunn, "The Saint's Legend as *Mimesis*: Gallican Liturgy and Mediterranean Culture," *Medieval and Renaissance Drama in England*, 1 (1984), 13-27.

[10]Richard C. Trexler, "Florentine Religious Experience: The Sacred Image," *Studies in the Renaissance*, 19 (1972), 18-21.

[11]Karl Young, *The Drama of the Medieval Church* (Oxford: Clarendon Press, 1933), I, 520-24; II, 199-219. The music for the Fleury *Lazarus* is transcribed in Gregorian notation by E. de Coussemaker, *Drames Liturgiques du Moyen Age* (1860; rpt. New York: Broude, 1964), pp. 220-22, and in modern notation by Fletcher Collins, Jr., *Medieval Church Music-Dramas: A Repertory of Complete Plays* (Charlottesville: Univ. Press of Virginia, 1976), pp. 189-239.

[12]Young, *Drama of the Medieval Church*, I, 451-83. For musical notation, see Coussemaker, pp. 195-203; Collins, *Medieval Church Music-Dramas*, pp. 63-88; and William L. Smoldon, *Peregrinus (The Stranger): An Acting Version* (London: Oxford Univ. Press, n.d.).

[13]See the versions of the *Visitatio Sepulchri* contained in the *Regularis Concordia* and the *Winchester Troper*; texts printed by Young, *Drama of the Medieval Church*, I, 249-50, 254-55. A phonograph recording of the *Winchester Troper* version has been prepared by the Schola Gregoriana, directed by Mary Berry, under the title *Anglo-Saxon Easter* (Archiv 413546-1).

I have not given any notice here to plays of the Virgin Mary or the *Planctus Mariae*; see Young, *Drama of the Medieval Church*, I, 492-518, and II, 225-57.

[14]Ibid., II, 219-24; musical notation transcribed by Coussemaker, pp. 210-15, and Collins, *Medieval Church Music-Dramas*, pp. 241-58. The Fleury music-drama should be compared to the English vernacular saint play on the topic of the Conversion of St. Paul; see the discussion in my article, below, on the English saint play.

[15]Young, *Drama of the Medieval Church*, II, 222.

[16]Ibid., II, 224. For comment on the staging of this drama, see especially Cynthia Bourgeault, "Liturgical Dramaturgy," *Comparative Drama*, 17 (1983), 132-35; rpt. in *The Fleury Playbook: Essays and Studies*, ed. Thomas P. Campbell and Clifford Davidson, Early Drama, Art, and Music, Monograph Ser., 7 (Kalamazoo: Medieval Institute Publications, 1985), pp. 152-55.

[17]Luba Eleen, *The Illustration of the Pauline Epistles in French and English Bibles of the Twelfth and Thirteenth Centuries* (Oxford: Clarendon Press, 1982), pp. 85-95. Cf. Fletcher Collins, Jr., *The Production of Medieval Church Music-Drama* (Charlottesville: Univ. Press of Virginia, 1972), pp. 172-81.

[18]Eleen, *The Illustration of the Pauline Epistles*, fig. 139.

[19]Ibid., fig. 143.

[20]Ibid., fig. 149.

[21]Ibid., figs. 152-71.

[22]Young, *Drama of the Medieval Church*, II, 307-60. For transcription of the music, see Coussemaker, pp. 83-92, 100-04, 109-15, 123-34, and Collins, *Medieval Church Music-Dramas*, pp. 281-95. Two of the plays, the *Tres Filiae* and the *Iconia*, have been recorded by the Studio der Frühen Musik under the musical direction of Thomas Binkley (Reflexe 1C-065-30-940 Q).

[23]See my treatment of the English saint play, Lynette R. Muir's survey of the French examples, and Kathleen Falvey's analysis of the Perugian saint play as an example of the genre in Italy, below. For the German saint play, see David Brett-Evans, *Von Hrotsvit bis Folz und Gegenbach* (Berlin: E. Schmidt, 1975), 2 vols., and for Spanish, see N. D. Shergold, *A History of the Spanish Stage* (Oxford: Clarendon Press, 1967).

[24]*Beunans Meriasek: The Life of Saint Meriasek, Bishop and Confessor: A Cornish Drama*, ed. and trans. Whitley Stokes (London: Trübner, 1872); and *The Life of Meriasek: A Medieval Cornish Miracle Play*, trans. Markham Harris (Washington: Catholic Univ. of America Press, 1977). For commentary on this play, see also Robert T. Meyer, "The Middle-Cornish Play *Beunans Meriasek*," *Comparative Drama*, 3 (1969), 54-64; Charles Thomas, *Christian Antiquities of Camborne* (St. Anstell: H. E. Warne, 1967), pp. 21-40; and Merle Fifield, "Folk Understandings and Misunderstandings: Narrative Unity in *Beunans Meriasek*," forthcoming in the Proceedings of the Third International Colloquium on Medieval Drama, Dublin, 1980.

9

[25]*The Life of Meriasek*, trans. Harris, p. 116; see also Harris' note (ibid., pp. 140-41) and Stokes' edition, pp. 248-49.

[26]G. H. Doble, *The Saints of Cornwall*, I (1960), 132.

[27]Meyer, "The Middle-Cornish Play," pp. 54-55, citing a footnote added by R. Morton Nance to Doble's *Saints of Cornwall*, I, 111n.

[28]*Beunans Meriasek*, ed. and trans. Stokes, pp. 266-67; see also *Life of Meriasek*, trans. Harris, pp. 16-18. On Cornish rounds as locations for staging medieval plays, see A. C. Cawley, "The Staging of Medieval Drama," in *The Revels History of Drama in English*, ed. Lois Potter, I (London and New York: Methuen, 1983), 14-19.

[29]*The Staging of Religious Drama in Europe in the Later Middle Ages*, ed. Peter Meredith and John E. Tailby, Early Drama, Art, and Music, Monograph Ser., 4 (Kalamazoo: Medieval Institute Publications, 1983), pp. 11-12.

[30]Ibid., p. 141.

[31]See especially John Phillips, *The Reformation of Images: Destruction of Art in England, 1535-1660* (Berkeley and Los Angeles: Univ. of California Press, 1973).

[32]See Clifford Davidson, "T. S. Eliot's *Murder in the Cathedral* and the Saint's Play Tradition," *Papers on Language and Literature*, 21 (1985), 152-69.

Persona in *Cantilena*:
St. Nicholas in Music in Medieval Drama

Clyde W. Brockett

The medieval 'saint play' has been defined as a genre roughly synonymous with 'miracle play.'[1] This genre, which concerned itself with the life, martyrdom, and miracles of a particular saint, began in Latin and in time conflated vernacular texts with the Latin ones. Music was a *sine qua non* whenever a play, spawned by the liturgy, appeared in connection with the saint's feast, but both words and music extend beyond liturgical requirements into outright invention. By means of such artistic enrichment, those persons accorded heroic stature by the Church were personified beyond static form; dramatizations, in effect, became the complements and enactments of their cult. Viewed according to subject and identified by the name of the saint conveniently listed in Karl Young's *The Drama of the Medieval Church*, the following repertory with music is at hand. In honor of Mary, there are plays on the Presentation, the Annunciation, the Purification, and the Assumption; for St. Paul, there is the representation of his Conversion; for St. Nicholas, his miracles associated with the Three Daughters, the Three Students, the Jew's Image, and the Son of Getron are extant; the *Planctus Mariae*, which includes the personages of the three Marys with St. John, is a touchstone of medieval artistic productivity; there exist, finally, some remnants of a play concerning St. Agnes.[2] This repertory of saint plays spans three centuries beginning c.1150, and certain traditions such as the Assumption from Elche in Spain have persisted even to the present day.

11

Continued popularity was perhaps assured by verisimilitude, often an elusively measurable degree of sacredness or secularity within the drama. Indeed, both secular and sacred are naturally manifest in the plays as had been the case in their charter documents, the combined Old and New Testaments and pertinent *acta sanctorum*. These appropriately reflect life and death, the corporeal and spiritual while fostering the *imitatio* of a saint in mundane affairs through actions which, proverbially, speak louder than words. Thus a passage from a sermon of Maximus of Turin (fifth century), read for the Matins Office of St. Nicholas, seems to express the theological basis of the saint play:

> Virtutum ejus gratia, non sermonibus exponenda est, sed
> operibus comprobanda
> (For his virtues' sake, not to be exhibited in sermons, but to
> be established in accomplishments.)[3]

It is to the extant music-dramas of St. Nicholas, which treat the saint's acts and miracles, that this paper will now turn, since, as we have seen, these plays are nearly unique in presenting a post-biblical saint.[4]

St. Nicholas, as Karl Young reported, is twice distinguished by medieval authors. He is, first of all, the only saint whose *acta* furnish sufficiently fertile—and thereby dramatically represented material—for more than a single plot. Second, he enjoys the greatest popularity of any saint in Christendom.[5] The four legends dramatized in the Fleury Playbook, albeit reduced from many circulated *miracula*, provide not only text but also the music and apply a kind of lyrical logic not in evidence in many of the other liturgical dramas that are currently extant.[6] It follows that textual-musical details would be handled with the exactitude which would come from personal familiarity with (or observation of) the *persona* in history or legend.

At the same time, liturgical chant finds itself intentionally paraphrased in these twelfth-century "scores." The ability of the playwright-composer to adapt as well as to invent is demonstrated by his handling of the more traditional aspects of this drama. Yet, when we depart from the specifically Christologic dramas and examine the Nicholas cycle in particular, we find less tendency to quote any liturgical chant. Instead, the music adheres only to the *style* realized in the tonal modes of Gregorian plainsong. Motives sung by the characters, although interrelated, diverge from "unacted" liturgical music—*cantus*—to a point beyond discernable paraphrase. Thus they engender a different monophony, often termed *cantilena*. Because music made to characterize is frequently the salient transmitting agent of liturgical drama, one ought to find that melody and character cohere no less than the components of their music achieve coherence.

In the first play of the Fleury tetralogy, *Tres Filiae*, the character of St. Nicholas remains neutral because the music, after the first episode, remains unchanged for the remainder of the drama—a play which includes his appearance in accordance with his legend. However, in the second play of the cycle, *Tres Clerici*, the saint becomes more of an individual, but even then only at his fourth speech. This, specifically designated as his *oratio*, is set to a change of melody. In my musical analysis I suggest that the new melody at the juncture of the *oratio* may have been introduced on aesthetic grounds.[7] But could it have been St. Nicholas' personality that warranted more succinct definition here?

Metrically, the prayer of St. Nicholas is undistinguished; it follows the decasyllabic measure, iambically, with the coupe or caesura between the fourth and fifth syllables. "Aer" must be separated by a hiatus into the dissyllable confirmed by its music, rendered in Example 1:

Example 1

Pi – e De – us, cu–jus sunt͜ om – ni – a,͜

13

ce – lum   tel–lus, a–er, et__ Ma – ri– a,__

ut resurgant . is – ti__ pre–ci– pi – as,__

et hos ad__ te clamantes au – – di – as!__

Melodically, the piece also is certainly far from unique. Its upward skip at the beginning, D-a, is symptomatic of the first tonal mode whose frequent incipits of D-a- -a are like a kind of motto. In fact, with recourse to the thematic index of David Hughes and John Bryden's *An Index of Gregorian Chant*, one readily uncovers a whole corpus of plainsongs which assume and stereotype at least the first eight distinct pitches;[8] two specific specimens are compared to the *oratio* in Example 2:

Example 2

Oratio Sancti Nicolai

Pi– e De – us, cu–jus   sunt__ om – ni – a,__

Hymn (*LU*, p. 1259)

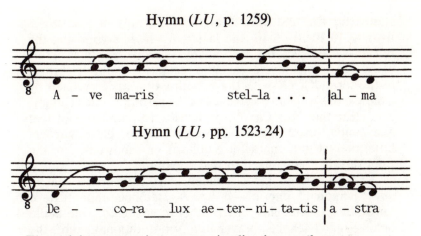

A – ve ma–ris___ stel–la . . . |al – ma

Hymn (*LU*, pp. 1523-24)

De – – co–ra___ lux ae – ter– ni– ta–tis |a – stra

Thus plainsong, or its specter, is alive in *cantilena*.

Considered from the standpoint of prosody, the same upward leap helps to set the iambic rhythm in motion with its second pitch, the higher, receiving a natural accent. In the last word, "audias," the melisma on "au-" has the sound of a litany, though it is separated from the Litany's environment of *Kyrie eleison*, *preces* (a form of sung prayers), and *letania* antiphon. The effect of a litany may have served to intensify St. Nicholas' own suffrages. On the other hand, it was customary for a cadential melisma to be introduced to complement as well as to embellish the textual-musical cadence.

For convenience in my analysis of form, I use the first letters of the alphabet to indicate verse rhyme scheme and the last letters to indicate musical rhyme scheme. In structural terms, St. Nicholas prefers the verse-form aabb and music XXYZ, both used throughout the *Tres Clerici*.[9] Here, the Y section cadences on a high pitch (a fifth higher): *ouvert*. The Z section, lower pitched, recalls some material from the X section and cadences on the same pitch as X: *clos*. This form is common in other medieval music-dramas: the complex *Daniel* play uses something similar in its octosyllabic hymnic *Conductus referentium vasa ante Danielem* ("Conductus of those bringing the bowl before Daniel").[10] The

15

stanza for the first chorus of the *Prudentes* in *Sponsus*—usually 10 10 10 · 5 10, the last two verses comprising the refrain—preserves the textual rhyme aaaB, rhyming internally. Yet its melody repeats and recapitulates the X phrase, in the form XXYX with the recapituation of X prefixed by a phrase to set the five syllables of the refrain.[11] Accordingly, it is clear that *Tres Clerici*, by hewing to paradigms of text and melody used in other contemporaneous plays, garners little interest in a character emphasis or "showcase" of the saint through recognized formal apparatus.

These commonplaces indeed leave little to be said of any "personal" imprint—*persona*—stamped upon text or music by St. Nicholas where he is represented. One could believe that Nicholas' prayer in a non-traditional genre, the hymn (instead of some psalmic, collectary, or lectional intonation more truly representative of an *oratio*), might have been designed to cast this saint as a liturgical nonconformist. Yet Jesus himself, he who in the words of St. Thomas Aquinas "keeps the feast its rites demand,"[12] is allowed verse set by non-liturgical *cantilena* in the Latin-language bistrophe "Amen dico" (4+4:7) followed by the Aquitanian-language tercet "Alet chaitivas!" in the *Sponsus* play. Incidentally, the *Pater noster* itself, though paraphrased in hymn and processional antiphon, is not to my knowledge assigned to Christ in dramatic representations of the age of the Fleury cycle. Nor does *Christus* alias *Sponsus* act in his biblical *persona* when he conjures an inferno into which demons hurl the *fatuae*.

Could the rhythmic "prayer" uttered by the St. Nicholas of *Tres Clerici*, then, be attributable to the prevailing goliardic aesthetic of the Three Scholars drama? Might the intellectuality of a metric "academic" setting not better personify one conversant with students? Indeed, in its context of supplication, not thanksgiving, for the lives of the dead students it is a stranger as a hymn. In the Einsiedeln version, the final speech of the saint does revive the students. There is merit in suppositions of modern scholars that *Tres Clerici* has a goliardic background; St. Nicholas projects well against it.

In the *Imago Sancti Nicolai*, we find the saint singing the same melody which the entire final two-thirds of *Tres Filiae* had used. It is, most interestingly, the same as the motive of the son of Getron which will be considered at length. I quote the three instances of this *cantilena* in Example 3:

Example 3

a. *Tres Filiae*

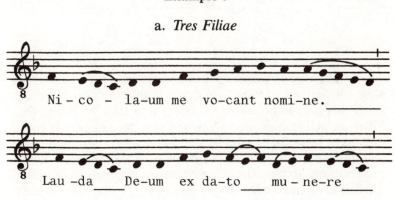

Ni – co – la–um me vo–cant nomi–ne.____

Lau –da____De–um ex da–to__ mu – ne–re____

b. *Imago*

Quid pro – phan– i, quid no–ta re – con – di – tis?_

Quid de – men– tes, ut ves–tra di – vi – di – tis?_

17

c. *Filius Getronis*

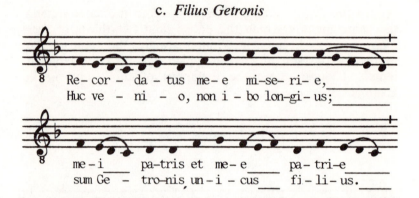

Re- cor - da - tus me - e mi-se- ri - e,
Huc ve - ni - o, non i - bo lon-gi - us;

me - i pa-tris et me - e pa- tri - e
sum Ge - tro-nis, un - i - cus fi - li - us.

If liturgical placement is any indication, the *Imago* would have introduced (rather than copied) this melodic formula, since this play is linked to the Mass and thus precedes *Tres Filiae*, which is assigned to Vespers of 6 December.[13] It could thus have been St. Nicholas' true leitmotif, rendering its use less curious than at first would seem to be the case. It has been surmised that the playwright intentionally continued the formulas in repetitious fashion in *Tres Filiae* for the sake of pleasant affect.[14] But the formula could have served to identify the several personages in *Tres Filiae*, including St. Nicholas, pursuant to its identification of the saint exclusively, earlier in the day, perhaps in the earlier composed play. This may also best explain the events of the "action," which do not appreciably differ, and the saint's attempt at anonymity as giver of dowries to the *pater* for each of his *tres filiae*.

In the *Imago Sancti Nicolai*, iconography assumes an obviously significant role in delineating the *persona*. At least one scene of this miracle, depicted in a stained glass panel in Rouen Cathedral, shows what looks more like a statue than a portrait of the bishop, *imago* having both meanings. It is the Jew praying to his statue of the saint. Fig. 1 shows this thirteenth-century panel, which is placed along with other thirteenth-century and fifteenth-century glass in the far left and left of center lancets of the St. Severus Chapel window.[15]

The white image is smaller than the Jew praying before it; the figure on the pedestal appears to be recessed in its niche far enough to look, in perspective, proportionately smaller than its mortal counterpart. Is it possible that the Fleury playwright used the convenient *imago* itself as its *dramatis persona* or, better, its *dramatis titulus*? Indeed, the scanty rubrics do not disallow any conceivable staging, nor does the text deny any personification of the image. Indicative, perhaps, is the Jew's tongue-lashing without physical harm attempted upon the play's "statue" in the Fleury Playbook, while in Hilarius' text, which is, of course, without musical notation, the image does sustain an actual thrashing. Hilarius seems to have intended this abused effigy to be "represented by another living person," as borne out by the rubric, which specifies *persona iconiae*.[16] But in the absence of melody, *persona* through music is a chimera, an *argumentum ex silentio*. Still, in the Fleury musical version the iconodule is asleep when his statue could have stepped down to consummate the miracle, not yet awake when the saint returns. Night is the time for this action, while daybreak is the time set by the Jew for effectuation—and the time which Nicholas sets for the thieves not to divulge his manifestation to them lest *they* get the whipping post for their entire misdeed. These are transformations of contemporary custom.[17]

The parallel to the election and liturgical activity of the boy bishop or *episcopellus* is virtually inescapable. Not only is the stained glass figure at Rouen small, but he is also unbearded and looks exactly like a boy. Descriptions of the *episcopellus* are divided as to which of the boy's ritual "Offices"—6 December, the Feast of St. Nicholas, or 28 December, Holy Innocents' Day—developed earlier, or whether both customs appeared at approximately the same historical moment. Indeed, the Feast of Fools, allied with the Innocents, was known to John of Avranches (Rouen) in the late eleventh century.[18] E. K. Chambers found documentation favoring St. Nicholas' Day dating from at least the thirteenth century to be manifold. In Salisbury Cathedral, a thirteenth-century "dwarf effigy of a bishop" is even found.[19]

19

Because references to music—supervised, so to speak, by the *episcopellus*—are in context of the liturgy with its *cantus* and not of *cantilena*, proof of "personification" of the boy bishop is not forthcoming. Although the requirements for consolers' roles are similar in both the *Slaying of the Holy Innocents* play and the Nicholas play of the *Son of Getron*, the *cantilena*-like treatment in the former is dissimilar to the *cantus*-like treatment of the same roles in the latter. With respect to *persona*, on the other hand, I see no reason why the *episcopellus*, a chorister and selected for his acumen displayed in both liturgical and musical matters, should not have played the role of the saint. I would advance beyond the opinion of Richard Donovan who holds that the choir boy's activities merely "bordered upon drama."[20]

This "casting"(!) of St. Nicholas is important for its possible effect on the music of the play. Although the character of St. Nicholas seems to be dramatically identical throughout the tetralogy, as Collins claims, it is by no means musically stabilized.[21] Nor is the music conventional. In the first half of the saint's lengthy address to the robbers of the *imago*, all sentences are questions, yet they unexpectedly progress downward through the uncommonly broad range of an octave in an unorthodox and non-rhetorical setting. In fact, of fifty-six questions in the medieval music-drama repertory which includes the *Imago* where a question is approached at any prior point only from above, only one case extends to a greater interval (to a ninth) and one other as far as an octave.[22] Much more natural to speech would be the question inflected, hence sung, upwards. One therefore observes that this particular musical portrayal allows the saint latitude and depth of speech as well as, especially, appreciable license with the interrogative mood when these are compared to the practice in other plays.

The last play in the St. Nicholas cycle, perhaps intended to be second in order by dint of its liturgical assignment, poses a serious problem to any musical personification of the patron: the saint sings nothing. Instead, he unceremoniously transports the kidnapped son of Getron in this play of the same name back to his home. It is this *puer* to whom the saint's theme of *Tres Filiae* and *Imago* is now assigned. But in this transfer, the leitmotif may have been not merely a character designation but also more a kind of symbol, as the concept of *leitmotif* itself infers. There are two themes, both of which seem to transcend the boy's *persona* to symbolize, in one instance, the church of St. Nicholas from which he was stolen away and, in the other, the saint himself.

In discussion of the music of the Fleury Playbook, I found that the melody assigned and designating *puer*'s mother, Euphrosina—a melody sung once only by *puer*—is more a *cantus* than a *cantilena*. It resembles both psalmody and antiphony of the sixth tonal mode and apparently symbolizes the consistent role of the suppliant, Euphrosina, with part of her *preces* actually inside the "Church of St. Nicholas."[23] But the boy, snatched from this same site, sings the leading motive to himself ("secum") at the point of consummate hopelessness almost as another prayer for, in this instance, liberation by death. Example 4 quotes the boy's chant-like formula with its text:

Example 4

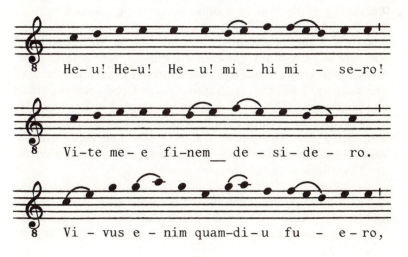

He- u! He-u! He - u! mi – hi mi – se-ro!

Vi-te me- e fi-nem__ de - si-de - ro.

Vi - vus e - nim quam-di-u fu - e-ro,

21

li-ber-a-ri__ ne - qua-quam_ po-ter-o.

Collins terms this thematic relationship between *puer* and Euphrosina an "umbilical effect."[24] But perhaps it is a cord which extends beyond natural *mater* to *mater ecclesia*. Indeed, the "Church of St. Nicholas," erected at the eastern end of the *puer*'s native Excoranda, owed its existence to God's favor of a son, "Adeodatus," and to the parents who honored St. Nicholas and his cult. One might even extend the prayerful motive from Church to saint proper.

In his other guise, *puer* speaks cogently and devotedly, as would befit the saint himself, in his rebuke of the kidnapper-king's Apollo worship. These deeply committed sentiments are expressed aloud in the wicked Marmorinus' presence. They also help to establish the time of the action: the anniversary of St. Nicholas' *Eve* which, after a full year's lapse, only this pious boy could characteristically call to mind. None of the previous researchers attracted to *Filius Getronis*, from Marius Sepet on, has noticed that near the beginning of the play in dumb-show the righteous family go "to the Church of St. Nicholas, as though for celebrating his feast."[25] That the youth is made not only so to remember 5 December in his devoutness, worthiness, and intelligence, but also to sing a *cantilena* associated in other dramas with the saint is, I believe, intentionally symbolic on the part of the playwright. The *cantilena*, earlier quoted in Example 3c, is thus, not surprisingly, one symbol of the saint in *Imago* and *Tres Filiae*. In a sense, the *cantilena* does represent Nicholas as a character in the *persona* of a *puer* before *puer*'s tacit restitution by the *deus ex machina*.

The part performed by *cantilena* in dramatizing *persona* is again here as discernable as it is conclusive. Even though the term *persona* is avoided by this playwright, his synonym *in similitudinem* generates interest in counterparts in music, in similitude of words, music, and personae throughout the repertory of medieval music-drama.

Excursus on the Cult of St. Nicholas at Angers

The following aggregation and interpretation of facts bears solely on the possibility of a cult of St. Nicholas and not directly on the origin of the Fleury Playbook. The earliest documentation regarding St. Nicholas in Germany or France is a poem by Raban Maur for the dedication of Fulda Abbey in 818.[26] It is reported that the St. Nicholas cult was implanted in Germany by Theophano, the Greek queen of Otto II, in the tenth century;[27] it thereupon was probably well diffused in Lorraine. Before the time of the Fleury Playbook, the Fleury Abbey library contained evidence of the cult, including the *Vita* by Joannes Diaconus, a St. Nicholas hymn contained in a tenth-century manuscript, and a sermon for St. Nicholas' Day by Hildebert, Bishop of Le Mans and Archbishop of Tours (d. 1139).[28]

The interest of the Normans in specially honoring St. Nicholas throughout their fiefs—in Calabria-Sicily, in England, and in Normandy-Maine—was considerable. The *Iconia Sancti Nicholai* had been, arguably, written in Calabria around 1000 A.D.[29] The colony established by Norman seafarers in Sicily could have introduced Byzantine customs there as early as 1017. But the Office of St. Nicholas composed in Rouen and presumed to be the one which circulated so widely in Normandy dates only from around 1030.[30]

The feature which all of these dates, except for that of Hildebert's sermon, have in common is the fairly great separation of their origin from the appearance of the full-fledged St. Nicholas plays; the evidence, so intelligently amassed by Otto Albrecht, suggests no cogent continuity from the eleventh century to the mid-twelfth century. Nor do these facts lend strong support for fixing the origin of the St. Nicholas collection of the Fleury Playbook somewhere in the Loire River basin from Fleury down, the only determination which all scholars presently seem to agree upon.

The following data allude to another St. Nicholas "center" in the Loire region, Angers, and to a possible intermediary, Pope Urban II. In 1089, this pope visited and confirmed the site of the saint's reinterment at Bari. He is even claimed to have single-handedly positioned the bones in a reliquary prepared for future visitations.[31] Pope Urban's itinerary through France in 1095-96 succeeded in instituting a number of Roman subtleties of ritual and protocol. *Mutatis mutandis*, it is possible that some non-Roman liturgical device was brought to *his* attention, though I as yet have found no record of such a consequence resulting from the visitation at St. Martial and Limoges over Christmas in 1095. On the other hand, Urban was not in Norman-controlled lands north of Italy at the proper liturgical season to witness such a special *ordo* as an eleventh-century dramatization based on the life and legend of St. Nicholas.

Significantly, however, on 10 February 1096 Urban did consecrate the monastery of St. Nicholas on the outskirts of Angers, possibly confirming a Nicholas cult there, in the presence of Count Fulk of Anjou and the most influential of the regional hierarchy.[32] This papal act was accompanied by the bestowing of public mention and pardons for an entire year to the worshippers at this monastery.[33] Moreover, Urban's secretary, Milo, a monk of St. Alban's, records that this dedication in France had majority approval in Rome.[34] And this activity was occurring possibly less than a half century before the assembling of the Fleury Playbook. After visiting Angevin shrines, Urban proceeded to Sablé, on the border of Anjou and Maine, where he confirmed the privileges and possessions to Natalis, Abbot of the Monastery of St. Nicholas of Angers.[35] Urban also conferred benefices "for the grace of those who visit the same basilica on the anniversary of its dedication."[36]

For three days during Lent, we find Urban being received, according to Mabillon's *Analecta*, with the *sacrosanctum hospitium* at Le Mans.[37] This honor, apparently reserved for the most revered of guests, was later advocated for strangers by the aforementioned Hildebert, as yet Arch-deacon of St. Julian's at the time of Urban's coming; the same kind of honor was involved in the contemporary Christian interpretation of the Emmaus Supper celebrated in liturgical drama.[38] Before returning to Rome, Urban was at Vendôme for ten days, also at Orléans, but not at Fleury. However, it was at Tours that Urban's ministry in the Loire region climaxed with the council over which he presided, with its extravagant mid-Lenten *Laetare* Sunday Procession at St. Martin's which featured waving a golden rose and a crowning with palms, *more Romano*.[39]

Important information bearing on the question of relics has quite recently surfaced. While searching at Angers very recently for documentation for the present Excursus, I found in MS. 121 of the Bibliothèque Municipale of Angers, on folios 149ʳ through 168ᵛ, a pertinent history of the Monastery of St. Nicholas, whose site I had visited across the Maine River on a hill overlooking the city.[40] In addition to evidence of an eleventh-century cult of St. Nicholas, this manuscript contains a group of his miracles—not plays, though with several speeches unfortunately different from those in the extant dramas—including the Daughters, Students, and Getron legends, but not the Jew and his treasure. Moreover, considerable space is devoted to the miraculous healings which took place at St. Nicholas' shrine and the lure to many living at great distances from Angers. The manuscript dates from the twelfth century; its *raison d'être* is chiefly to chronicle the "Translation of Saint Nicholas," as its writer titles it. I quote the passage which concerns the relics of the saint:

> Up to this day the feast of the day instituted by our elders, dearest brethren, has received the name of the Translation because of veneration, specifically of the relics of the sacred body of our glorious patron, blessed NICHOLAS, which, formerly, revered Count Goffrid deposited in this place. Beforehand, his father, Fulk, had founded this church [first founded in 1020] and had placed in it a certain site for the aforementioned holy relics.[41]

25

This manuscript goes on to tell us (fol. 163ᵛ) that it was Abbot Baldric who situated the relics in the monastery. Judging from this account which involves Count Fulk, sponsor of Pope Urban's visit, we could assume that the abbey had awaited its "patent," the saint's relics, for perhaps a century, as it had awaited papal confirmation for roughly three quarters of a century.

In summary, there are in these details both arguments for and against considering the lower Loire area to be a late tenth-century or early eleventh-century field for the implantation of a cult of St. Nicholas. Arguing in favor are the following: (1) Urban II had been indirectly connected with the translation of St. Nicholas at Bari; (2) Urban, in or around Campania, Apulia, and Calabria, was in regular contact with Norman-influenced practitioners of a St. Nicholas cult; (3) Urban confirmed the Church of St. Nicholas of Angers in person in 1096; (4) this St. Nicholas' was a monastic, not a secular basilica; and (5) Goffrid, only shortly after this papal confirmation, brought actual relics of St. Nicholas' "sacred body" to a repository for their veneration at Angers. Arguing against are the following: (1) there is no mention of a special *ordo* such as would indicate a liturgical drama, although records surveyed are not of the *De officiis* type; and (2) the date of consecration of St. Nicholas' monastery, 10 February, is asynchronous with the probable performance days of dramas, appropriate cultic responses, which would be 5-6 December or perhaps 28 December. But this discrepancy of liturgical day certainly does not preclude the possibility of the institution of commemorative representations at the monastic basilica at Angers. This sort of commemoration of St. Nicholas, in fact, seems altogether likely.

NOTES

[1] E. Catherine Dunn, "The Origin of the Middle English Saints' Plays," in *The Medieval Drama and Its Claudelian Revival*, ed. E. Catherine Dunn, Tatiana Fotich, and Bernard M. Peebles (Washington, D.C.: Catholic Univ. of America Press, 1970), p. 1. This propounds the interesting thesis that the farced lection, furnishing as it does both liturgical contexts and actual texts related to feted saints, carried the spores of miracles, only a few of which now survive. The compilation and cataloguing of extant texts have been the monumental achieve-

ments of Karl Young, *The Drama of the Medieval Church* (Oxford: Clarendon Press, 1933), 2 vols.

[2]Not catalogued by Young in *The Drama of the Medieval Church*, but with reason, these latter fragments, now in the Vatican Library (MS. Chigi V, 151), are a mélange of material on St. Agnes, probably dating from the Renaissance period but assembled in relatively recent times; see Theodore Gérold, *Le Jeu de Saint Agnes* (Paris: E. Champion, 1931).

[3]From the Common of Confessor Bishops, *Breviarium Monasticum pro omnibus sub regula S. Patris Benedicti militantibus, pars hiemalis* (Malines, 1939), p. 117.

[4]Plays on the life and legend of St. Nicholas *without music* are extant from Hildesheim (Young, *Drama of the Medieval Church*, II, 311-16, 324-30) and Einsiedeln (ibid., II, 335-37) as well as in the version of the *Iconia Sancti Nicolai* by Hilarius (ibid., II, 337-43).

[5]See Young, *Drama of the Medieval Church*, II, 308.

[6]The Fleury Playbook is contained in Orléans, Bibliothèque Municipale MS. 201; the St. Nicholas dramas appear on pp. 176-205. For facsimiles, see G. Tintori and Raffaele Monterosso, eds., *Sacre rappresentazioni nel manoscritto 201 dell Biblioteca municipale di Orleans*, Instituta et Monumenta, Ser. I: Monumenta, No. 2 (Cremona, 1958), and Thomas P. Campbell and Clifford Davidson, eds., *The Fleury Playbook*, Early Drama, Art, and Music, Monograph Ser., 7 (Kalamazoo: Medieval Institute Publications, 1985). The music and text of the St. Nicholas plays are transcribed in E. de Coussemaker, *Drames liturgiques du Moyen Age* (1860; rpt. New York: Broude, 1964), pp. 83-142, and Fletcher Collins, Jr., ed., *Medieval Church Music Dramas: A Repertory of Complete Plays* (Charlottesville: Univ. Press of Virginia, 1976), pp. 283-395.

[7]C. W. Brockett, "Modal and Motivic Coherence in the Music of the Fleury *Playbook*," *Comparative Drama*, 16 (1982-83), 352; rpt. *The Fleury Playbook*, ed. Campbell and Davidson, p. 42.

[8]David G. Hughes and John R. Bryden, *An Index of Gregorian Chant* (Cambridge, Mass.: Harvard Univ. Press, 1971), II, 349. The abbreviation *LU* in this *Index* and herein refers to the *Liber Usualis* (Tournai, 1947), which has preserved a fair number of plainsongs in their corpus.

[9]William L. Smoldon, *The Music of the Medieval Church Dramas* (London: Oxford Univ. Press, 1980), pp. 264-65.

[10]Coussemaker, *Drames liturgiques*, p. 59. Its meter is 8 8 . . . with refrain 8 7. The melody of the verse 2 repeats verse 1, and verse 4 repeats verse 3, to produce AA BB in the music. A good example of the sequence-like fifteen (sixteen) syllable verses to music without intended musical rhymes is the *Conductus Daniel* ("Congaudentes celebremus," p. 62) 8 7 double, with its AA BB (actually AA transposed up a fifth) AA CCC (fifth higher) AA BB AA effecting the perfect embryo of the so-called sonata rondo of the eighteenth century: ABACABA.

[11]Coussemaker, *Drames liturgiques*, p. 2. Verse 2 of Stanza II varies, ABBA, probably because names are uttered in verse 2 ("Virgini," "Betleem") assimilating it to verse 3 ("flum Jorda"). Verse 3 may have called for oratorical delineation on an identical pitch (here F) as seems to justify the monotone for five or six syllables in all the stanzas (I: "espos," "Jhesu"; III: "Deu"; IV: "Io," referring to the names in I). More about the dichotomy of meter and the so rhythmic modes in music in this piece is found in my review of William L. Smoldon's *Music of the Medieval Church Dramas* in *Ars Lyrica*, 2 (1983), 45-48, and in the practice found in the *Conductus Daniel*. Also in *Daniel* the sequence-like (aa bb...xx) *Conductus Regine*, 4+5 4+6 occurs (Coussemaker, *Drames liturgiques*, p. 53) without any addition to its AB ostinato form.

[12]From the Communion hymn *Pange lingua gloriosi Corporis mysterium*; see *LU*, p. 951; cf. *Hymns Ancient and Modern* (London, n.d.), p. 513 (trans. E. Caswall, J. M. Neale, and others).

[13]Brockett, "Modal and Motivic Coherence," p. 359.

[14]Fletcher Collins, Jr., *The Production of Medieval Church Music-Drama* (Charlottesville: Univ. Press of Virginia, 1972), pp. 204-05, 225.

[15]Around 1300 this framed scene was refitted, along with the other *belles verrières* dating from around 1225, possibly with new bordering but without alteration to any scene, into the St. Severus Chapel window. One might assume its original location to have been the St. Nicholas Chapel. The glass is illustrated in Collins, *Production*, fig. 60, and in Georges Ritter, *Vitreaux de la Cathédrale de Rouen: XIIIe, XIVe, XVe, et XVIe siècles* (Cognac, 1926), pp. 38-39, referring to Pl. e.8. Interestingly, the Rouen glass includes representations of a beardless Nicholas for his Consecration at Myra (e.7), the Jew about to beat the image (e.4; heads restored), and the resuscitation of the three students (a.7). An undramatized episode, dealing with the false Diana, depicts the saint bearded, as far as the eye can determine (e.1). I am grateful to Professor Madeline Caviness for this information. See also Louis Réau, *Iconographie de l'art Chrétien*, III: *Iconographie des Saints*, Pt. 2 (Paris, 1958), pp. 985-86.

[16]Smoldon, *Music of the Medieval Church Dramas*, p. 266, considered this possibiity as an attempt by Hilarius to simplify his setting.

[17]"Ne deprensi mane a populo, me indicante, digni patibulo penas solvatis." Note the Greek-oriented spelling "prophani" for "profani" at the beginning of this reprimand and threat.

[18]E. K. Chambers, *The Mediaeval Stage* (London: Oxford Univ. Press, 1903), I, 338.

[19]Ibid., I, 353. See also the article by L. Petzoldt in *Lexikon der christlichen Ikonographie*, ed. Engelbert Kirschbaum and Wolfgang Braunfels, VIII (Rome: Herder, 1976), 45ff.

[20]Richard Donovan, *The Liturgical Drama in Medieval Spain* (Toronto: Pontifical Institute of Mediaeval Studies, 1958), p. 65. Because of what he considers the *episcopellus'* tangential relationship to the drama, Donovan deals no further with his manifestations in Spanish churches while admitting that they were legion and relegating a list of documents treating the Boy Bishop to an Appendix (pp. 191-92).

[21]Collins, *Production of Medieval Church Music-Drama*, p. 209.

[22]To the ninth: the question "Cur me dabit . . ." in *Daniel*. See Coussemaker, *Drames liturgiques*, p. 65. Even here, the approach from above is far more circuitous than in *Imago*. To the octave: the question "Ubi consolacio mea?" from *Planctus Mariae*. See ibid., p. 285.

[23]Brockett, "Modal and Motivic Coherence," pp. 357-58. The term *preces* (sing. *prex* is rare) actually figures in Euphrosina's suffrages of verse 79; see Young, *Drama of the Medieval Church*, II, 354.

[24]Collins, *Production of Medieval Church Music-Drama*, p. 234.

[25]"Ad ecclesiam Sancti Nicolai, quasi ad ejus solemnitatem celebrandum"; Collins (*Medieval Church Music Dramas*, p. 368) even translates this "as if to *a* solemn celebration" (italics mine).

[26]Otto E. Albrecht, *Four Latin Plays of the Twelfth Century* (Philadelphia, 1935), pp. [13-14].

[27]A. G. Gibson, "St. Nicholas of Myra," *New Catholic Encyclopedia* (New York, 1967), X, 454.

[28]Albrecht, *Four Latin Plays*, p. [5].

[29]Ibid., p. [43].

[30]Ibid., p. [15].

[31]Theodore Ruinart, "Vita Beati Urbani II," in *PL*, CXLI, 59-60: "Ibi beatissimi antistitis ossa pontifex [Urbanus] propriis manibus in locum parati aditi collocavit."

[32]*PL*, CLI, 192.

[33]*PL*, CLI, 194: "idem apostolicus, et edicto jussit ut in eodem termino, quo dedicationem fecerat, indictum publicum celebraretur unoquoque anno apud Sanctum Nicolaum, et septima pars poenitentiarum populo convenienti ad illam celebritatem dimitteretur."

[34]*PL*, CLI, 195: "ad quam [dedicationem] magna senatus Romani pars occurrisse dicitur."

[35]*Epistola*, CLXXV; *PL*, CLI, 447-49.

[36]*PL*, CLI, 196: "Februarii 14, Urbanus Sablolii . . . confirmat privilegia et possessiones

monasterii Sancti Nicolai Andegavensis . . . multa beneficia decernit, uti diximus, in eorum gratiam, qui eamdem basilicam die anniversario ejus dedicationis inviserint."

[37]*PL*, CLI, 196: "inter omnes antecessorum suorum titulos solus universalis papae et sacrosancto hospitio honoratus fuerit."

[38]F. C. Gardiner, *The Pilgrimage of Desire* (Leiden: Brill, 1971), pp. 80-81; see also my "Easter Monday Antiphons and the *Peregrinus* Play," *Kirchenmusikalisches Jahrbuch*, 61/62 (1977-78), 31n.

[39]*PL*, CLI, 202: "Etenim processio in qua pontifex rosam auream gestare solet, hac ipsa Dominica mediae Quadragesimae, in qua scilicet *Laetare* canitur," and "[media] Quadragesima in ecclesia beati Martini more Romano corona palmarum se coronasse, ibique missam ad altare Dominicum celebrasse."

[40]See A. Molinier, *Catalogue général des manuscrits dans les Bibliothèques publiques de France*, XXXI [1898], 222, 233.

[41]Fol. 162[v]: "Hodierne diei festivitas a nostris maioribus instituta fratres karissimi translationis nomen accepit ob venerationem videlicet reliquiarum sacri corporis gloriosi patroni nostri beati NICHOLAI, quas olim allatas andecavorum comes reverendus goffridus in hoc loco reposuit. Cuius pater fulco hanc ecclesiam prius fundaverat atque in ipsa de sanctis supradictis reliquiis positionem quandam posuerat."

The Middle English Saint Play
and Its Iconography

Clifford Davidson

In his important investigation of the final years of medieval drama, Harold Gardiner correctly notes that we have
considerable reason to wonder about the small number of
extant "miracle plays" or, to be more exact in our terminology, saint plays (as opposed to the so-called "mystery plays"
on biblical topics) from medieval England.[1] Aptly Gardiner
calls attention to the prevalence of the miracle or saint play
in France where the Miracles of the Virgin Mary were especially present "in great numbers." Further he points to
the English guild dedications to saints in England which
"would lead us to anticipate that a large number of plays on
the miracles and virtues of these popular saints would have
come down to us."[2] Dramatic records from English sources
which have survived do indeed indicate that the miracle or
saint play may even have been the most important genre in
the repertoire of the English medieval stage. For the earliest
example of a saint play to be recorded in England, a play on
the subject of St. Catherine which was identified specifically
as a "miracle" play and staged c.1110—i.e., very nearly contemporary with the *Sponsus* from St. Martial of Limoges[3]—
there is no evidence whether the presentation was in English,
in French, in Latin, or in a macaronic text as in the case of
the *Sponsus*.[4] But it is very clear from the evidence that
subsequently there was a great flourishing of this genre up
to the time of the Reformation. Yet very little remains of
what was then a healthy tradition of playing the lives and
sufferings of the saints on the medieval stage.

I

Where the dramatic records have been thoroughly searched, as in the case of York, there is considerable ambiguity concerning the nature of productions which may have been part of the saint play tradition. The St. George Procession and Riding at York thus illustrate the point. While the riding of St. George, recorded in 1546-47 to 1558[5] but clearly much older (a reference in a will dates it back to 1503[6]), most certainly had elements that qualify it as dramatic, this civic exercise, sponsored by the Guild of SS. Christopher and George until its suppression, could in fact have been closer to a folk drama than to an actual performance of a saint play. We shall, however, return to the question of St. George Ridings and their relation to the saint play later in this study.

There is also considerable ambiguity with regard to the York play of St. James, recorded in the will of William Revetour who in 1446 left the playbook to the St. Christopher Guild in the city; it was described by its former owner as a certain "ludum de sancto Iacobo Apostolo in sex paginis compilatum."[7] We do know that this guild could have been involved in devotion to St. James, since the guild utilized the Guild Hall and facilities for several days surrounding the feast day of St. James on 25 July, a day which also was St. Christopher's Day.[8] It is not impossible that the play was designed for presentation during these festivities. But whether the play was a separate presentation on the life of St. James, which could even have included episodes linked to the cult of the apostle at the famous shrine at Compostella in Spain, we cannot in the end know, and there is even the possibility that the play was not a separate play at all but rather a segment of the lost York Creed Play.[9] In another instance, a supposed letter from Henry VIII translated and printed by J. O. Halliwell in *Letters of the Kings of England* (1848) claims to report a sixteenth-century production "of a religious interlude of St. Thomas the Apostle, made in the said city [of

York] on the 23rd of August now past" which allegedly helped to fuel rebellion, apparently in c.1535.[10] Unfortunately, the letter, reported to have been seen in the Rawlinson manuscripts at the Bodleian Library, cannot now be located and there is clear doubt concerning its authenticity.[11] Furthermore, this letter would not necessarily indicate a separate play of St. Thomas the Apostle but very likely the Scriveners' pageant from the Corpus Christi cycle—a play extant in a separate manuscript in addition to its presence in the York Register.[12]

We are, however, on firmer ground when we turn to the play of St. Denys that was left to the church of St. Denys, York, in 1456 by Robert Lasingby, "clericus parochialis S. Dionisii Ebor," in his will.[13] Described as "ludum oreginale Sancti Dionisij," the play is clearly connected with the cult of this saint which we would expect to have been strong in a parish church dedicated to him. Nothing, of course, has come down to us concerning the events of the saint's life dramatized in this play, though the narratives describing his life and the iconographic evidence would suggest a rather spectacular theatrical action. Glass in a window in the church of St. Denys contained glass (now in storage) from 1452-55 or precisely contemporary with the play of St. Denys in Lasingby's will.[14] This glass, which unfortunately is mutilated, shows the saint in the vestments appropriate to a fifteenth-century bishop as he holds his head, which still wears a mitre (fig. 2). There was also an image of the saint in the same church from at least as early as 1460, as the will of John Cawton, who died that year, indicates.[15] Presumably this image, like the painted glass, represented the saint as a bishop, beheaded but carrying his mitred head.[16]

St. Denis or Dionysius, the patron saint of France but extremely popular also in England, was commonly believed to have been converted by St. Paul; later he became a missionary and eventually the Bishop of Paris who, along with two companions Rusticus and Eleutherius, was beheaded there for his faith.[17] An eleventh-century manuscript illumination now in the Bibliothèque Nationale, Paris (MS. Lat. 9,436, fol. 106ᵛ), shows the last Communion of the saint; before the altar he receives the host from Christ himself who appears with a cross nimbus.[18] According to Caxton's translation of the *Golden Legend,* St. Denys and his companions were beheaded with axes "by the temple of mercurye. . . . And anone the body of saynt denys reysed hymself vp, and bare his hede betwene his armes as thangels ladde him two leghes from the place/ whiche is sayd the hille of the marters/ vnto the place where he now resteth by his election/ and by the purueaunce of god."[19] The saint's relics were, of course, present at St.-Denis northeast of Paris which was the center for his cult, though devotion to him was particularly widespread. More than forty churches were dedicated to him in England, and, for example, his martyrdom figures in such a prominent sculptural cycle as the early fourteenth-century bosses in the cloister of Norwich Cathedral, where he is shown in the North Walk being executed before the Emperor (seated, with scepter) and two retainers (fig. 3). Here the saint kneels while the executioner raises his right arm to cut off his head (the sword is missing) and with his left hand he holds onto the mitred head. Next to the kneeling figure is the decapitated saint carrying his head, while at the right is the west doorway of a church, presumably St.-Denis, where a cleric in a surplice is welcoming him.[20]

Some further theatrical possibilities may be suggested by an illumination, also from the fourteenth century, by the Master of the Queen Mary Psalter in Bodleian Library MS. Canon Misc. 248, fol. 45ᵛ.[21] At least four scenes are concerned with St. Denys, illustrating his final communion, his beheading by three executioners who swing swords and an axe at the kneeling saint, his appearance before the door of the church at St.-Denis, and his entombment in his shrine, an episode in which his head with its halo is held up for veneration. While less valuable for our purposes than examples in the visual arts from the actual locale where the York play of St. Denys was written and performed or from a date very close to the presumed original performances of the drama, the Norwich bosses and the manuscript illumination nevertheless are indicative of some directions that the action of the play might have taken. As a cautionary note, it should be indicated that there is no solid evidence that any of the extant examples in the visual arts, either at York or elsewhere, were influenced in the least by theatrical presentations of the story of St. Denys.

With regard to the theatrical presentation of the York play of St. Denys, we know certainly only the existence of the playbook and the fact that the parish would have had the means to present such a play. In 1449 a reference in the City Chamberlains' Rolls indicates payment of 4d "to 2 players of the parish of St Denys,"[22] which is proof of theatrical activity associated with the parish. The theatrical presentation of a play of this saint, probably staged for the regular feast day of the saint in the York calendar on 9 October, could well because of the date have been indoors, perhaps even inside the church of St. Denys itself. But here we are entering the region of speculation—a region which is, of course, extremely tempting in the light of the tantalizing glimpse that we are able to gain from the dramatic records and from iconographic evidence.

II

In addition to their devotional intent, one purpose for the presentation of saint plays by parish players would seem to have been the practical one of fund raising. Thus at Braintree, Essex, local players staged at least three plays on the lives of saints in the third and fourth decades of the sixteenth century to raise money for renovations and improvements to their parish church of St. Michael. Braintree was, to be sure, well situated for such ventures, located as it was on the pilgrim routes to Bury St. Edmunds and to Walsingham.[23] The eighteenth-century Essex historian Philip Morant reports that these theatrical efforts helped to build a new porch, new aisles, and perhaps a new roof.[24] Concerning the plays, Morant writes:

> Toward the charge of this building, besides the large contributions of the inhabitants, there were three plays acted in the Church; the first of which was St. Swithin, in 1523. The second of St. Andrew, on the Sunday before Relique Sunday, in 1525. The third and last was of Placy Dacy, alias St. Ewestacy, acted in 1534. These were not only for pleasing the eye and ear, but likewise for satisfying the belly; for which great provision was always made, the accounts of the Church wardens of those times were very particular and exact in. After the Reformation the Church wardens not only lent the players garments, but at last sold them for 50s. [in 1579] and the playbooks for 20s. [in 1571].[25]

Churchwardens' accounts indicate that the plays produced in 1523, 1525, and 1534 were successful, raising about £15 16s altogether.[26] Additionally, these accounts further report a "play in Halsted Church," perhaps by the Braintree parish players, in 1529, though no receipts appear to have been noted.[27]

Apparently the parish itself took the lead in organizing the plays of 1523 to 1534, since a number of vicars served Braintree during this period; Nicholas Udall's incumbency dates from later, 1537-44, and in any case he was very likely a non-resident vicar who was merely represented by a curate.[28] The choice of St. Swithin for the first venture seems entirely logical, for this Anglo-Saxon saint was known to have been very active as a builder of churches.[29] This play and the next, on the life and legend of St. Andrew, who was also regarded as a builder of churches,[30] are described as having been actually "acted in the Church," the first on "a Wednesday" and the second one week before "Relique Sunday" or two Sundays after Midsummer. That there was a connection with Relic Sunday may be surmised, since on that Festival the relics in the churches were especially honored.

That the producers were able to learn from their experiences in putting on these plays, or at least were able to attract larger audiences with each of the performances, is indicated by the records in the churchwardens' accounts, which itemize increasing profits for each of the plays. The most successful was the last, dramatizing St. Eustace, a legendary saint who was converted to Christianity upon seeing a stag with a crucifix between his antlers. He was the patron of hunters, quite popular in England though only a very few churches were dedicated to him.[31] His martyrdom, however, probably was a sufficiently spectacular event upon which to base a somewhat sensational ending for a play designed to raise money as well as to excite devotion: at the conclusion he is put to death by the Emperor Hadrian for refusing to sacrifice to idols, and this is effected by placing him along with his family into a bronze ox heated by fire.[32]

A different kind of practicality mixed with devotion is evident in a play presented by a craft guild rather than a parish, in this case an Anglo-Irish example from Dublin,[33] which would suggest a practice that is likely to have been widespread. In this instance, a play on the subject of SS. Crispin and Crispinianus, the patron saints of shoemakers, was presented at Christmas time in 1528 before Thomas Fitzgerald, Earl of Kildare, by the Shoemakers of Dublin.[34] The dramatic records in their fragmentary state seem to corroborate the theory that such plays by craft guilds giving publicity to their crafts' patron saints might have been the rule rather than an exception. Possibly further light on this matter will be provided through the ongoing research in records being done under the auspices of the Records of Early English Drama project.

III

At Lincoln, the earliest recorded saint play is that of the Apostle Thomas first noted in the cathedral account books in 1321-22, which indicate that 9s 9d were paid for expenses associated with a play "de Sancto Thoma didimo" presented during "the time of" Easter—more specifically, as the accounts for later years prove, during Easter week, on Easter

Monday,[35] when the *Peregrinus* would have been appropriate because the lessons for the day included the Emmaus story[36] which was contained in the liturgical play that also drama- tized Thomas' doubts.[37] We learn from the accounts for 1326-27 that this drama was further presented in the nave of the cathedral,[38] another reason to doubt that it would have been a vernacular saint play. The *Peregrinus,* in Latin, is perhaps best known in a version from a French cathedral, Beauvais, where it illustrated the desire of the clergy to use all the resources of the singing men and boy choristers to produce a devotional effect that would also bring credit to their cathedral. This drama, which represents a different genre from the vernacular plays, shifts between liturgical expression and theatrical representation to create an effect that is very moving to an audience capable of understanding the tradition. It is not, however, popular drama, since it is aimed at persons sufficiently knowledgeable in the Latin lan- guage and familiar with the conventions of this genre. In any case, the Lincoln play of St. Thomas, which was probably a *Peregrinus* drama, was mentioned again in 1368-69[39] and may, as Virginia Shull suggests, have been retained longer.[40]

The play of St. Thomas of the early- and mid-fourteenth century must, therefore, have been quite radically different from the saint plays which appear in the Lincoln dramatic records of the middle of the fifteenth century. These later dramas probably did not neglect the devotional element which had surely dominated the earlier play, but their subject mat- ter by itself suggests opportunity for sensational and popular spectacle which would please the people, particularly since the plays were without question now presented in their lan- guage of English. Reliance on the stories of saints whose feast days fall in late July or early August may argue for presentation on St. Anne's Day, which seems otherwise to have been an important date in Lincoln.

The earliest of these plays, treating the life of a favorite saint, St. Lawrence, whose relics were reported by Bede to have appeared first in England when the pope made a gift of relics to King Oswy of Northumbria, is noted under the years

1441-42.[41] It is not clear under whose auspices at Lincoln this play was staged, nor can we know with exactitude what episodes were included from the historical and legendary lives of this saint, who was a deacon martyred by being roasted on a gridiron in 258 A.D. in the persecution promoted by Valerian.[42] A date on or near his feast day, on 10 August, would have been an excellent time for a theatrical presentation out of doors, though again we are not able to determine, of course, anything of the original staging of this lost play.

Lack of certainty cannot, however, prevent us from knowing some of the scenes that would likely have been staged in the Lincoln play of St. Lawrence. Scenes in the visual arts showing the martyrdom of the saint are fairly common, as in the early fourteenth-century painted glass in a nave window in York Minster where a torturer is working a bellows to fan the flames beneath the victim and others hold pokers (fig. 5).[43] M. D. Anderson calls our attention to a window in the church of St. Lawrence at Ludlow (rebuilt c.1445-55 with glass of the same date, and hence very nearly contemporary with the Lincoln play) which illustrates the saint's life much more completely, giving visual substance to the events included in his legend more or less as they are recorded in the *Golden Legend*.[44] Unfortunately, although Miss Anderson believed the window to have been "restored" according to the pattern of the medieval original, we can hardly be so sure about all details of the design. It was "remade" by David Evans of Shrewsbury in 1832, and actually is a copy which, though reputed to have been carefully done by Evans, was patterned after medieval glass that was in very bad condition. In 1684, Dineley reported that the glass contained in it "the whole History of St. Lawrence, to whom this Church was dedicated," without noting any damage,[45] but in the early eighteenth century it was severely treated in a disastrous releading. According to Thomas Wright, prior to Evans' work the window "was particularly defaced and wantonly broken, so much so indeed that the various subjects displayed could with difficulty be traced; though it appears, from a date near the top of the window, to have been repaired in a bungling manner about 1720, when the numerous fractures it then contained were filled with common painted glass, quite opaque."[46] However, modern examination of the window has indicated that while Evans had a good sense of fifteenth-century design, the color fidelity at least is poor.[47] Nevertheless, in spite of the obviously questionable nature of the restoration, careful examination of this window may suggest many scenes that would have been present in a play from the mid-fifteenth century on the subject of the same saint.

As presently arranged, the glass illustrating the life of St. Lawrence at Ludlow reads from the top of each light downwards, beginning with the left light, where St. Lawrence kneels before his confessor in the sacrament of Confession, receives ordination as a deacon (from St. Sixtus), accepts treasure from the son of the deceased emperor, gives money from a bag to poor and disabled persons, is imprisoned, is taken before the Emperor Decius, causes idols to collapse before him, is returned to prison, and, in prison, restores the sight of the blind Lucillus. These subjects on the whole are confirmed by the inscriptions, as are the subjects in the second and third lights. The second light contains the following: St. Lawrence, in prison, converts his jailer, whose keys are on the ground; in response to the Emperor's demand that he should turn over his wealth to him, he brings to him a group of the poor and disabled persons whom he has previously helped; the angry Decius beats them with a mallet, and they fall; instruments of torture are displayed by the Emperor before the saint; the nearly nude saint is led out to be stoned; he is scourged before the Provost Valerianus; he is beaten with clubs and trampled upon; he is tied to a pillar and beaten with whips; and, also attached to a pillar, his flesh is torn with flesh hooks. The third, or right hand, light contains the remaining subjects: St. Lawrence, again attached to a pillar, is tortured with red-hot irons; he is placed on a grid-iron, while men stoke the flames and Christ, in the background, looks on; he is buried; a deacon allows a chalice to fall and break; St. Lawrence reappears to a clergyman with a sprouting piece of wood; he directs the distribution of bread and wine; the saint shows a church dedicated to his memory; three figures (pilgrims?) pray in a church; and, finally, workmen are erecting a church.[48]

Too much reliance, of course, must not be placed on an iconographic program such as we have in this window: for example, the choice of the number of scenes would be determined by the matter of the design of the window rather than by the number of scenes that would have been included in a drama designed for presentation by contemporaries of the glass painter in this instance. But the usefulness of having iconographic evidence will be evident (or, rather, the lack of such evidence will immediately be seen as a problem) as soon as we turn to the next miracle plays appearing in the records for Lincoln, first a play of St. Susannah ("Ludus Sancti Susanni") in 1447-48 and then a play of Robert of Sicily ("ludus de Kyng Robert of Cesill") in 1452-53.[49] The first of these subjects is reported by M. D. Anderson to be extremely rare in England, and the second, which to be sure is more of a pious romance than a proper saint's legend, is totally unrepresented in English art of the pre-Reformation period.[50] St. Susannah, whose cult was linked with another Roman martyr of the third century, St. Tiburtius, is not included in the *Golden Legend,* and perhaps would have been regarded as an appropriate topic for a play mainly because of her feast day, shared with St. Tiburtius, on 11 August, which is very near to the feast day of St. Lawrence, on 10 August, suggesting regular performances at or near this time of year. An alleged letter from the Chester mayor and Corporation printed by John Payne Collier purports to describe a play of Robert of Sicily from a somewhat later date than the Lincoln date: "It is callyd Kynge Robart of Cicylye, the whiche was warned by an Aungell whiche went to Rome, and shewyd Kyng Robart all the powre of God, and what thynge yt was to be a pore man; and thanne, after sondrye wanderynges, ledde hym backe agayne to his kyngdome of Cicylye, where he lyved and raygned many yeres."[51] Doubtful as this alleged account may sound, the play was verifiably presented at the High Cross in Chester in 1529-30.[52]

In 1454-55, a play of St. James (*Ludus de Sancto Jacobo*) was staged at Lincoln,[53] presumably focusing on the life and legend of St. James the Great and perhaps on or near his feast day of 25 July. Here the iconography of the early thirteenth-century (or even earlier) wall paintings at Stoke Orchard, Gloucestershire,[54] seems to be only vaguely suggestive of what might have been staged elsewhere in the country and more than two hundred years later. Yet can the extensive dramatic possibilities suggested by this wall painting—especially the saint's confrontation with a magician, Hermogenes, who was converted miraculously—be denied? Nevertheless, it would seem that more directly relevant is an English alabaster reredos which has been at Compostella in Spain since 1456; this item illustrates the calling of James by the sea of Galilee, Christ speaking to the apostles, the preaching of St. James, the saint's martyrdom, and the translation of his body,[55] though surely more scenes, including events reported in the *Golden Legend,* would have been chosen in any dramatization of the life of this popular saint to whom at least 414 churches were dedicated in England.[56] No doubt some considerable emphasis would have been placed on the idea of St. James as a pilgrim—an idea associated with Compostella, where the presumed relics of the saint were located and to which great numbers of English pilgrims flocked. (Indeed, Stoke Orchard, which has been noted above for its early wall paintings showing more than thirty scenes from the life and legend of the saint, was on the pilgrimage road to Bristol where many of the pilgrims embarked for Spain.[57]) Interest in this saint may well have been spurred by the presence of relics in England—e.g., the saint's hand at Reading[58]—but more to the point would seem to be the identification encouraged between the pilgrim in the Middle Ages and the figure of St. James. And many from the city of Lincoln did indeed go on pilgrimage to such locations as Santiago, Rome, and Jerusalem—journeys in which they would dress as St. James is commonly dressed (with a scallop shell emblem, staff, and scrip) in representations of him in the visual arts across England in the late Middle Ages. Hence the statutes of the Fullers' Guild at Lincoln required that a guild member setting out on such a pilgrimage should be accompanied outside the municipality to the Eleanor Cross without Bargate and given a minimum of a halfpenny by each of the other members.[59] Other guilds at Lincoln had similar ordinances, which further provided for a joyous welcome home by the guild brethren; the Rule of the Guild of St. Anne also required them to meet him at the Cross without Bargate and to accompany him first to the cathedral and then to his home.[60] The individual participates in the pilgrimage and its experience of liminality[61] on behalf of the community of the guild, in which he has surrendered his function upon leaving; by thus participating in the pilgrimage, the individual also links both himself and his brethren to the figure of St. James whom he is imitating. Likewise the play of St. James must have been designed to lessen the distance between the individual viewers and the saint himself, who is thus invoked in devotional experience to bridge the gap between humanity and the order of divinity—an act which is possible because, as the Church insisted, *the saints are with God, and God is everywhere.*[62]

The final saint play recorded in the dramatic records at Lincoln is a play of St. Clare (*ludus de Sancta Clara*) in 1455-56,[63] again possibly on or near the saint's feast day, in this case 12 August. Since she was founder of the Order of Poor Clares or Minoresses, the play may suggest Franciscan involvement in the production of these plays, though there is for this no hard evidence. As head of a community who was essentially contemplative and who, in spite of one exciting episode when she repelled an invading army by holding up the Host before it, spent her entire life in her convent at Assisi, she is indeed a curious choice as the topic for a play, though again the placement of her feast day may have been the determining factor (perhaps in addition to possible Franciscan involvement) in the preparation of a play on her life and its staging in Lincoln.

The likelihood of Franciscan involvement in the medieval drama, including the saint play, has been surveyed by David L. Jeffrey,[64] who points to Franciscan dramatic activity on the continent and especially to the practice of the *sermo semidrammatico*. Jeffrey further takes note of a St. Nicholas "pleye" which was to be presented following the homily "yf ye wollet stille be" according to a sermon in Middle English verse in Cambridge, Trinity College MS. 323, fol. 26.[65] Such involvement by the Friars Minor is possibly further underlined by a poem that attacks them with extreme bitterness written by a Wyciffite—a poem that perhaps makes reference to a play of St. Francis which could only have been staged by the Franciscans with the help of their followers. "On the Minorite Friars," which appears in British Library Cotton MS. Cleopatra B.ii, fol. 64ᵛ, presents a confused account of the life of St. Francis as it may have been dramatized. It would appear that the author had seen a dramatization of the stigmatization of St. Francis, the saint's appearance to Pope Gregory IX ("I sawe a frere blede in middes of his side,/ Bothe in hondes and in fete had he woundes wide,/ To serve to that same frer, the pope mot abide," ll. 26-28), and his appearance to his followers at Rivo Torto.[66] Lawrence J. Craddock has established that these scenes must have been based on the life of the saint in the *Legenda Maior* of St. Bonaventure.[67] As such, it illustrated both those scenes that are familiar in art—e.g., a cross "fer up in the skye/ And festned on him wyenges, as he shuld flie" (ll. 7-8)—and some scenes that are unknown in surviving examples of English art. For example, the apparent hanging of Christ "on hegh on a grene tre/ With leves and with blossemes that bright are of ble" (ll. 8-9) that puzzled and offended the Wycliffite writer is explained as a representation of the seraph that appeared to St. Francis in a vision—a scene that was illustrated in an illumination by Matthew Paris, who places the seraph on a little platform and against a cross made up of tree trunks (fig. 6).[68] That legendary elements associated with the life of St. Francis were popular, however, may be suggested by the scene in painted glass at

St. John's Church, Winchester, discovered in 1852 (but shortly thereafter destroyed) which showed St. Francis leading the blessed into the bliss of heaven.[69]

The apparent presence of plays of St. Francis in England at least indicates Fanciscan interest in theatrical presentation with the intent of inspiring a devotional response and of contributing to the stature of the Franciscan order. At Lincoln, the appearance of St. Clare as the subject of a play presented presumably in the summer at a certain time (i.e., early August or for the feast of St. Anne in late July) as part of an annual series with other plays that would be appropriate for this season in other years argues strongly but not conclusively for the hypothesis that there was Franciscan involvement in the Lincoln saint plays of the middle of the fifteenth century.

IV

The late tradition that there was Franciscan sponsorship of plays at Coventry in the Middle Ages has been often noted,[70] though for this city we are not able to find any connection between the lost saint plays mentioned in the dramatic records and the Friars Minor. Indeed, the dramatization of the life of the Irish Cistercian monk—"the Play of St Christian played in the Little Park"—which appeared in the city annals of Coventry for the year 1505[71] could hardly have been a subject promoted by the friars. This reforming saint, an associate of St. Bernard at Clairvaux, was the abbot of the initial Cistercian monastery to be established in Ireland and later became Bishop of Lismore.[72] Neither was his feast day, 18 March, particularly appropriate to the kind of outdoor presentation that is suggested in the description of the location of performance as "in the Little Park," though as we shall see below a further document will indicate a more propitious date. Hardin Craig insisted that the records must be in error and that "Christian" or "seynt christean" must be a mistake for "St. Catherine";[73] however, the play was also noted in another document, the proof of majority

45

of Walter Smythe in the Public Record Office, which notes that a "great play" which was called "seynt christeans play" was presented in a field next to the city—a location called "lyttle parke" at Pentecost in 21 Henry VII, i.e., 1506.[74] Thus is the playing area localized as beyond Little Park Gate in the south outside the city, but the feast on which it was performed is additionally recorded—Pentecost, or a time which would seem to argue for local auspices rather than for a production by a troupe from elsewhere on tour.[75] In any case, the evidence seems to be that the play was spectacular and indeed memorable, though we are unable today to determine why this should have been so.

The other saint play recorded at Coventry is the drama on the subject of St. Catherine, a favorite saint for representation in the visual arts and on the medieval stage. This play was recorded as also having been performed in the Little Park but in 1490-91.[76] Quite likely, as R. W. Ingram seems to suggest,[77] there may well have been a connection between the play and the Coventry Guild of St. Catherine, founded in 1343 but later united with the Trinity Guild.[78] As the senior guild to which those of the rank of sheriff and above belonged,[79] it is hard to believe that this play was unimpressive if it was to honor one of the patrons of that guild. The cryptic reference in the records merely itemizing a saint play dramatizing the legendary life of St. Catherine in no way enables us to know precisely the content or the iconography of that play, though careful examination will allow us to understand the perimeters within which the medieval playwright and (presumably) the skilled amateur or professional theatricals would have worked to create their spectacle.

It is hard to say how early the cult of St. Catherine was fully established in England, but by the fourteenth century it appears to have been so widespread that veneration of her was to be found in all parts of the country.[80] In the early twelfth century, as we have seen, a theatrical presentation focusing on her life gives us the earliest record of a saint play in England: the play of St. Catherine at Dunstable, in Bedfordshire, in c.1110, which was described as a "play" (*ludus*)

46

or "miracle" ("quem 'Miracula' vulgariter appellamus").[81]
The episode, which is well known, is recorded because one
Geoffrey, who had borrowed choir copes from the abbey at
St. Albans for the play, had the misfortune to lose them in
a fire, and for reparation went into the monastery where he
later became the abbot. Possibly St. Catherine was made
especially popular because of the crusades,[82] which would
seem to have provided a source of her relics in England (e.g.,
the feretory "contenyng the fynger of saynt Katheryn yn a
long purse ornate with perles" at Lincoln[83]). Very possibly
of considerable importance for founding of the Guild of St.
Catherine in Coventry and for the presentation there of the
play on the subject was the presence in the city at the Cathedral Church of St. Mary (now totally destroyed) of "A
reliquie of Saynt kateryn / of Copper."[84] A chapel dedicated
to St. Catherine was located in St. Michael's Church (later
Cathedral) in the city, but this dedication is hardly unique,
with a great number of such dedications of chapels and of
churches as well dating from the Middle Ages in England. In
Coventry, the Chapel of St. Catherine had guild associations,
and an image of the saint is noted in the records of the Guild
of the Holy Trinity, St. Mary, St. John the Baptist, and St.
Catherine.[85] Further, the guild paid for keeping a candle before the image of the saint on her feast day, 25 November.[86]
The first recorded dedication of a church (and a hospital) to
St. Catherine was possibly Queen Matilda's foundation in
1148 near the Tower of London, in the locale of the present-
day St. Catherine's Docks.[87] From the thirteenth century,
extensive examples of representations of the saint's life were
present in the visual arts (e.g., twenty panels of painted glass
dated c.1285 in the Chapter House in York Minster, six panels
of glass of c.1308-20 in the nave of the same building, or the
wall painting dated c.1225 in the Chapel of the Holy Sepulchre in Winchester Cathedral where fives scenes were
shown).[88]

How spectacular the play of St. Catherine could have
been is illustrated in the pictorial cycle showing her life in
twenty-five scenes in the wall painting (fig. 7), now faded,

from the fourteenth century on the south wall of the south aisle of the church at Sporle, Norfolk.[89] Attention has been called to this wall painting by M. D. Anderson in her *Drama and Imagery in British Churches*. Her comments usefully summarize the events depicted from study of some nineteenth-century copies of the wall painting.[90] Fortunately, the wall painting has also been very thoroughly described by E. W. Tristram.[91] The story begins with a meeting between the Emperor Maximinus (with his Empress, at the left) and Saint Catherine (at the right) outside a temple where he is planning to sacrifice to idols. Next the saint appears, with her hand raised in protest, to interrupt the pagan worship itself, which is directed to an idol in the shape of a devil on an altar (center). The third scene illustrates her dispute with the Emperor, seated at the left. The Emperor is also present in the next scene, where he is seated at the left while St. Catherine overcomes the pagan philosophers brought in to argue with her. Then the pagan philosophers, now converted and encouraged by the saint who stands at the right, are burned; a furnace appears in the center of the scene, and an executioner behind. At this point the Emperor (enthroned) attempts to lure her with fair words, but, as the next scene shows, she fails to respond to his flattery and is led off by two jailers to prison. Her prison is described by M. D. Anderson as "the sort of stage property box with a large barred window in it that is familiar in alabasters,"[92] though such a building is more likely simply an artistic convention passed on from generation to generation through artists' model books.

Before the window of St. Catherine's prison is a figure which must be Porphyry, who is converted in the next scene along with two hundred further knights. In the latter scene, there is a half figure of Christ above, while Porphyry kneels below with the grouping of knights behind him. St. Catherine is then brought back to the Emperor, seated at the left, before whom she appears, naked to the waist and showing evidence of having been scourged. One of her torturers holds a whip. She is now condemned to be tortured by wheels which have knife blades attached, but in the crucial scene, which is central to her story and provides her with her emblem (see, for example, the image of the saint, probably from a reredos in the Whitefriars, Coventry, which typically includes the wheel as an identifying symbol[93]), the wheels break, having been shattered by angels sent to her assistance; Maximinus, at the left, has received a wound in the face from a fragment of a wheel, and other figures have additionally been hurt or killed. The Empress kneels to appeal for mercy for the saint, and in the next scene the Empress herself has been condemned, for she is being led away in captivity by the jailer. Thereafter we see the Empress, kneeling, being decapitated, and in a separate scene being buried by the chivalrous convert Porphyry, who does this charitable act by the light of the moon.

The martyrdom of the Empress initiates a series of scenes showing further martyrdoms, including the two hundred soldiers and also a single figure, apparently Porphyry. The bottom row opens with St. Catherine once again before the Emperor, and then she is shown between torturers, the one on the left sticking out his tongue and the one on the right with a grotesque nose and also an extended tongue. The next panel is symbolic, showing the soul like a small nude child in the control of devils. Then St. Catherine is led away, having been condemned to death, and in the following scene is shown kneeling in the center while the executioner raises his scimitar. Angels appear above right, ready to take her body away to Mount Sinai where she will be buried. The final scene shows pilgrims doing devotion to the saint at her tomb.

Naturally, the above description of a St. Catherine cycle at Sporle only indicates scenes that might have been present in the Coventry play, which likely would have been more complex or more simple than might be suggested by these wall paintings. Other cycles of wall paintings, many of them incomplete and damaged, present variable numbers of scenes.[94] Hence one example in Warwickshire, at Wootton Wawen, is so faded and indistinct that it is now impossible to see how extensive was once the series of scenes from the life of this saint.[95] In English alabaster carvings, St. Catherine was likewise a popular subject, but here the number of scenes was fairly standardized and limited. These, however, do provide some useful details that are worth noting. An alabaster[96] now in the British Museum (fig. 8) shows her refusing to worship the devilish idol, which stands on a pillar and holds something that looks like a brush over its shoulder; the Emperor has his bare sword raised in anger. In an alabaster owned by the Society of Antiquaries, the saint in prison appears with the Empress and Porphyry, to whom she has extended her hands; on the canopy is the dove which fed her with heavenly food during her imprisonment.[97] This carving may be a lost scene from the series from a reredos at Lydiate, Lancashire, which additionally includes the burning of the philosophers (one executioner has a two-pronged fork, while the Emperor has a demon crown[98]), the breaking of the wheels, the saint praying and encouraged by four female friends prior to her execution, her execution (her head is tumbling to ground from the body as the illustration shows the sword already having sliced through her neck, and hence the executioner is resheathing his sword while the jailer is identified by the keys attached to his club), and her entombment (two streams of oil miraculously flow from the side of her tomb). A final alabaster image in the series is the figure of the saint with a sword.[99]

The trial of the philosophers is additionally included in a set of six alabasters at Vienna, where the Emperor, seated cross-legged with his left foot on a cushion and holding a drawn sword, is attended by a fool with a bauble. St. Catherine and the five philosophers, who are appropriately dressed in coif, robe, and tippet, have their index fingers raised in a gesture that indicates making a point in argumentation.[100] In another scene, the burning of the newly-converted philosophers, the saint encourages the martyrs with a gesture formed by holding hands together with all fingers of the left hand extended but only the index finger of the right hand touching the middle finger of the left hand.[101] In the beheading scene in this series, the fool appears again (beside the block) as the saint is about to be beheaded, while an angel at the top already has a napkin with the soul of the martyr.[102]

Of course, though the above are extremely interesting when we begin to examine the details which are utilized in these representations of the story of St. Catherine, further examination of such details cannot provide certitude concerning the contents of the play at Coventry or of the other plays on her legendary life. They nevertheless give us invaluable evidence of how the story of St. Catherine was visualized in the later Middle Ages, though we can of course make no claims about a direct relationship between the plays and the scenes in the visual arts. Neither are other plays or pageants on the subject of this saint very helpful toward establishing a full description of the St. Catherine drama and its staging in the Middle Ages. The London play of St. Catherine performed in 1393 (perhaps, as Alan Nelson suggests,[103] at Skinners' Well) is merely mentioned in a fifteenth-century chronicle contained in British Library Add. MS. 565: "In this yere was the pley of seynt Katerine."[104] A pageant presented by the Journeymen Cappers as part of the Corpus Christi festival at Hereford, Herefordshire, in 1503 may have been no more than a *tableau vivant,* though there presentation is noted in the Corporation Register as involving "Seynt Keterina with tres (?) tormentors."[105] In any case, a pageant for the entry into London of Catherine of Aragon on 12 November 1501 turns out to be not very dramatic, though it is definitely of interest because of the apparent participation of young actresses. About 2 p.m. on this day the princess, then betrothed to Prince Arthur, came to London, where she was met at London Bridge by actresses, "oon representyng Saynt Kateryn, and that other . . . Saynt Vrsula, with dyuers livyng virgins. . . ."[106] St. Catherine's speech is additionally included—a monologue intended to make a favorable impression on the Spanish princess.[107] Another account reported in *The Antiquarian Repertory* (1807-09) indicated the presence of a "tabernacle" in the middle of the bridge with two seats, one of which was occupied by "a faire yong lady with a wheel in hir hand, in likenes of Seint Kathryn, with right many virgynes on ev'ry side of her," while above was a person playing St. Ursula "with her great multitude of virgyns right goodly dressed and arrayed." Above them both was "the pictour of the Trinyté." On the sides were six small censing angels.[108]

In London as elsewhere, of course, the cult of St. Catherine had been strongly established. For example, the London Haberdashers' Guild had been incorporated as the Fraternity of St. Catherine the Virgin in 1447-48, though her patronage of this guild apparently actually dates from at least as early as 1381.[109] There were also several religious guilds devoted to this saint, including one at St. Paul's dating from 1352.[110] At first the latter guild supported the cost of keeping a candle lighted in a chapel dedicated to God, the Blessed Virgin, and St. Catherine, and later a chaplain was retained for services. That the feast of St. Catherine was particularly important at St. Paul's as late as the time of Queen Mary is shown by an entry in the Diary of Henry Machyn, who reported a procession on the vigil of the feast "abowt Powlles stepull with gret lyghtes, and [before them an image of] sant Kateryn, and syngyng, with v[c]. lyghtes allmost halffe a noure, and when all was don thay rong all the belles of Powlles at vj of the cloke."[111] It was, of course, in the context of the medieval veneration of St. Catherine that the lost plays were produced as focuses for devotion to her. Like images which would bring her to view before the eyes of worshippers, the plays were designed to bring to sight a representation of one who is a heroine of faith now residing with God and thus available to be invoked by those who would call on her for aid. Indeed, this functioning of the cult of the saint is crucial for our understanding of the drama.

V

The great English saint whose cult was established with extreme rapidity following his murder at the altar of Canterbury Cathedral in 1170 was Thomas Becket, whose shrine for centuries attracted immense numbers of pilgrims, including that assorted group of folk of whom Chaucer wrote in his *Canterbury Tales*. As a story of martyrdom frequently dramatized and staged, the life of Becket has even plausibly been claimed by John Wasson as a principal example of a genre that formed the basis for the tragic form eventually established during the age of Elizabeth I and James I in the late sixteenth and early seventeenth centuries.[112] It is unfortunate that not a single play text on the life of this saint is extant, though this fact is not surprising in the light of the great hostility of the Reformers toward him because he was seen by them as a vigorous champion of a corrupt Roman Church against the national state and the crown. Indeed, Henry VIII's Injunction against him in 1538 declared him to be "a rebel and traitor to his prince" and ordered all images and pictures of him to be "put down" while his cult was to be utterly suppressed.[113] Lost plays on Becket most likely were much more numerous than the dramatic records at this date would seem to indicate. Nevertheless, as Professor Wasson has noted, "it is possible to surmise with considerable confidence what the St. Thomas plays were like."[114] There is, furthermore, some extremely enlightening information concerning plays of Becket in the dramatic records themselves. Then, to the evidence of the dramatic records and the literary narratives of the saint's life, the latter of which provide a story that is quite stable in its handling of incidents, we can further add information from iconography as it appeared in the visual arts following the martyr's death and terminating only with the suppression of his cult at the Reformation.[115]

The earliest recorded play of St. Thomas Becket is reported in 1384-85 at King's Lynn, where payments were noted in the chamberlains' account books for playing an interlude dramatizing his life ("Et de iijs iiijd sol' ludentibus interludium Sancti Thome Martiris").[116] M. D. Anderson plausibly suggested that this play might have been connected somehow with the Guild of St. Thomas which had been founded at Lynn as early as 1272[117] and which in particular celebrated the feast of the translation of the saint on 7 July with considerable elaborateness.[118] The date of 7 July would obviously have been much more appropriate for outdoor performance than the regular feast day of 29 December. That the guild was also interested in honor paid to the image of the saint is shown by the presence of a statue representing him before which lights were regularly provided. The image was in the parish church and perhaps placed in the Chapel of St. Thomas of Canterbury there.[119]

The popularity of St. Thomas of Canterbury in East Anglia is corroborated by the fifteenth-century procession on 7 July, the feast of his translation, at Norwich. This procession was especially associated with the Guild of St. Thomas in this city. Francis Blomefield reports that the feast days of the saint were marked by "grand Processions" and the playing of "Interludes . . . with good Cheer after them."[120] While no mention is made of a Becket play, such a drama would have been a distinct possibility.[121] At Mildenhall in Suffolk, however, there was "a play off Sent Thomas" staged "in the hall yard" in 1505 that certainly was a Becket play since the record of the play is found in an account book of the churchwardens for the Guild of St. Thomas of Canterbury.[122] In line with East Anglian practice, the "Sent Thomas day" on which the play was presented was most likely the feast of the translation of the saint, 7 July, rather than either the regular feast day or 1 December, the day of the archbishop's return from abroad where he had been in exile—a day which was sometimes commemorated in England.[123]

Finally, a curious reference in the churchwardens' accounts for 1539 in the Suffolk town of Bungay records a "seruyce of thomas beckytt" which at first sight would appear to have been a play.[124] Interestingly, Richard Charnell was paid two shillings for correcting the book, which initially may seem to suggest an attempt to make it acceptable to the authorities during this unsettled period when the government had in fact already suppressed the saint's cult. However, Ian Lancashire has plausibly argued that "Charnell was probably striking Becket's name out of the liturgy."[125]

In Kent, a play of Becket is possibly implied in the

chamberlains' accounts of the town of Lydd on the feast of
the translation of the saint by players from Ham as early as
1453-54,[126] but the most extensive dramatic activity focusing
on the life of the saint appears predictably to have been at
Canterbury itself. The documentary evidence indicates the
presentation of a dramatization of Thomas Becket from
1504-05 to about 1537-38,[127] a date which would mark the
official suppression of the cult, with a revival in 1554-55
under Queen Mary when the play or pageant was produced.[128] Fortunately, these records are extensive and
illuminating.

The expenses for the presentation of St. Thomas Becket
at Canterbury would seem to indicate a fully dramatic production, very likely something much more impressive than
the debased "show" which Giles Dawson thought was a de-
cadent survival of "an old St. Thomas play" at least for the
years between 1513 and 1538.[129] We learn from the civic
accounts[130] that boy actors may have been utilized, apparently playing the parts of the knights in 1515-16 and somehow
participating in the production in 1518-19. The saint-hero of
the play wore a mask and head-piece, described as "seinte
Thomas hede" and not surprisingly repainted frequently, as
well as gloves, which were replaced in 1513-14. Provisions
were made for further garments in 1519-20, including (possibly) a chemise ("chemer") made of white canvas "for seynt
Thomas" as well as a quantity "of blak tuke for the typpet."
A new tippet "of Buckeram" was provided in 1529-30. There
is mention of washing the saint's alb as well as the altar
cloths used in the presentation of the martyrdom of the saint.
A new cross was provided, presumably the cross-staff for
the archbishop, in 1530-31; the "croyser" noted in the accounts for the next year was clearly the *crosiarius,* Edward
Grim, who also was apparently a character that appeared in
the London dramatic records for the play of St. Thomas
treated below.[131] The knights' harness was also reported as
needing to be refreshed.

Some attention is given to the effects that were used in
the play, for example providing a clue to the use of stage

blood in the martyrdom since in 1504-05 and subsequently payments were made for leather bags for the blood.[132] The wounding of the saint in the head utilizing the false "hede" worn by the actor thus would have been not a scene for the squeamish to watch! A painted mechanical angel, apparently operated from wires by a mechanical contrivance or "vyce," was also used, and a person would be paid for operating or "turnyng" the contrivance. Less clear is a reference in 1515-16 to a "candell to lyght the turnyng of the vyce." Was this a convenience for the man who did the turning, or was the image of the angel lighted thus to achieve an effect? The pageant wagon itself was painted and gilt, and was fitted with painted cloths. If the references to the image of St. Thomas "vppon the Auter" in 1519-20 indicate the stage altar used in the martyrdom scene rather than an altar of St. Thomas in a chapel, we have indication of the decoration of the altar before which Becket was standing at the end of his life in the play. The accounts for this year record payment for painting "an ymage of our lady with ij angelles gylt" which would "hang ayenst" the image of the saint. The next year cloth was purchased for making a surplice for the "ymage," presumably of St. Thomas.

The martyrdom scene central to this production is also the most commonly represented point in the Becket story as it is illustrated in the visual arts, and indeed it is possible only to select a few examples that will illustrate the iconographic pattern established in the Middle Ages. For example, fourteenth-century painted glass in the tracery of a window in St. Lucy's Chapel at Christ Church Cathedral, Oxford, shows the knights, with shields and swords, at the right attacking the saint (headless since the Reformation) at the altar at the left; the attendant monk, Grim, is holding the archbishop's cross staff in his left hand beside Becket.[133] A roof boss at Exeter Cathedral shows the kneeling saint in the center receiving the first blow from a knight while the other three knights crowd behind; at the right, beside the altar and holding the archbishop's cross staff, is Grim.[134] A fifteenth-century alabaster in the British Museum likewise shows the martyrdom scene, with the four knights at the left (fig. 9). One knight has in this case thrust his sword into Becket's head, while a second knight is preparing to strike the second blow. Two further soldiers have their swords raised, points up. Grim stands at the right holding the cross-staff and a book.[135] An early sixteenth-century wall painting in the nave of the Guild Chapel at Stratford-upon-Avon illustrated the attacking knights as having faces darkened with anger.[136] In the fourteenth-century bosses in the cloister of Norwich Cathedral, Grim is attended by an angel, while at the same time the knights are attended by two devils.[137] A destroyed wall painting of the thirteenth century in St. John's Church, Winchester, uniquely illustrated one of the knights actually slicing off the top of the saint's head while an angel appears above to receive his soul.[138] In none of these examples from the visual arts is the conclusion of the martyrdom shown— i.e., the scene in which it is the cruel Hugh of Horsea, not one of the knights, who, placing his foot upon Becket's neck, knocked his brains about on the floor of the cathedral.[139] A boss in the cloisters of Norwich Cathedral, however, does present the murdered archbishop lying on the floor on the altar steps while several monks mourn him.[140] It is also a shame that no scene of the martyred archbishop, apart from his appearance in miracle scenes, remains at Canterbury Cathedral itself except a late fifteenth-century figure (in the northwest transept) of Becket wearing a chasuble over a garment of hair (part of which is a modern replacement) and holding a cross staff.[141]

The mechanical angel possibly is not, however, adequately explained merely by means of the iconography of the death of Becket. A clue to the likely role of this angel in the play may nevertheless at least tentatively come from another aspect of his iconography, the scene of his requiem Mass. This may be examined in an example contemporary with the Canterbury play—i.e., the glass originally in St. Wilfrid's Church, York, and now in the Chapter House of York Minster. As the tonsured celebrant kneels before the altar on which appears a chalice, an angel appears above

57

with a scroll. Two monks are grouped below before a book
on a desk. The celebrant's right hand is holding an open
book, while beside him is an acolyte. The important detail
for our understanding of the Canterbury play is the appearance in the scene of the angel with a scroll. In the *Golden
Legend,* the story is told of what happened as the clergy of
Canterbury Cathedral were preparing to chant *Requiem eter-
nam*: "whan the quer began to synge Requiem/ An angelle
on hye aboue began thoffyce of a martir: *Laetabitur iustus
[in Domino]*."[142] Quite possibly the mechanical angel represented this unearthly choir that appeared from the heavens, though of course such speculation cannot be susceptible
to proof. It would have been simple for earthly voices to
supplement the large puppet angel with actual music in the
scene.

A London production of a Becket show was also recorded in the Skinners' wardens' accounts for 1518-19. Payments this year included 3s 4d to Thomas Bakehouse "for
playing the Martyrdom of St. Thomas Becket with all the
properties both nights," 10d to Richard Ward "for bearing
the ladder for St. Thomas' pageant both nights, and for cord
and nails to mend the pageant by the way," 18d to Richard
Matthewe "for playing Gilbert Becket and for his clerk both
nights," 3s 6d to Robert Johnson for playing "Tracy the
Knight" and also to Robert Hynstok "for playing the Jewess
both nights," and 16d to John Mayne "for playing the 'Sowden' before the Martyrdom of St. Thomas." Richard Stabyll
was paid 8d for acting as the *crosiarius*. The wardens of St.
Giles were paid "for hiring a pageant," presumably a wagon
on which the play could be presented. Halle, a carpenter,
was paid for "making [Gilbert] Becket's prison" (there was
also a jailer), while William Dayly hired a mitre for the actor
who played Thomas to wear.[143] Clearly here the subject of
Becket's parentage was represented, following the account
that appears in Caxton's version of the *Golden Legend*.[144]
Gilbert Becket, the father of Thomas, had, while jailed on
his way home from a pilgrimage to Jerusalem, met a legendary Saracen princess (presumably the character identified as

the "Jewess" in the records of the London play), who followed him to London with the knowledge, according to Caxton, of only one word of English, "beket." Her arrival in
London is illustrated in the first of a series of illuminations
in the fourtenth-century *Queen Mary's Psalter,* fol. 282^v, where
she is shown with the servant of Gilbert who is named Richard, a character that had apparently been played by Richard
Mathewe's clerk in the London production.[145] Another
manuscript illumination in *Queen Mary's Psalter* (fol. 289)
shows the baptism of Becket's mother in St. Paul's Cathedral—a scene that is also shown in a painted glass panel
dated c.1530 from the series originally in the church of St.
Wilfrid, York. This panel is now in a window in the church
of St. Michael-le-Belfrey in that city.[146] The "Sowden" played
by John Mayne is surely her father, the "Soldan," from whom
Gilbert Becket has escaped during his travels; a third panel
now in St. Michael-le-Belfrey shows the saint's father kissing
his future wife goodbye after she has assisted him in his
escape, followed by another panel (obviously out of sequence in its present location) in which the jailer shows to
the Saracen prince the irons from which Gilbert and his servant Richard have escaped. This glass additionally shows the
marriage of the parents of the saint.[147] Further panels from
the same series now in the Chapter House of York Minster
provide illustration of nine additional scenes: Gilbert's arrival
in England, the journey of the princess to London by ship,
the birth of the saint, the saint taken to be educated by the
canons of Merton College, his ordination, his quarrel with
the king and imprisonment, his exile in Rome and the miracle
of the capon-carp, the saint's Mass before the Pope, and his
return to England.[148]

    The staging is hardly fully described in the records, but
we are able to learn from them that the prison was a portable
set or pageant that required six men to carry. The Soldan,
the knight William de Tracy, the jailer, and the "Jewess"
were assigned horses, and the amount of 2s 10d was paid for
attending them. The pageant stage, as we have seen, needed
mending along the way, and lighting was provided by "prick-

ets, torches, and tapers of wax." When the show was completed, the pageants had to be returned. It is only possible to guess at the use to which the ladder provided by Richard Ward would have been put, but could it have been used for the escape of Gilbert Becket from prison? Or would it have been used in the manner indicated by the *Hours of Etienne Chevalier* in the illumination illustrating the martyrdom of St. Apollonia—i.e., as a means of access to the stage area?[149] From the decription it is clear that we are dealing here with a fully dramatized saint play rather than merely with a *tableau vivant*.

VI

The play of St. George presents some very different problems since, as noted above, the distinction between folk drama and saint play is often extremely unclear from the evidence of the dramatic records. As early as 1473, Sir John Paston, in a letter to his brother John, complained about the loss of a servant, Kothye Plattyng, for "I haue kepyd hym thys iij yere to pleye Seynt Jorge and Robin hod and the Shryff off Notyngham."[150] This play would seem clearly to have been folk drama and not saint play, but the dividing line between the two genres is without doubt often open to question.

The sixteenth-century play of St. George at York, to which reference has been previously made in this chapter, was presented as part of the celebrations organized by the Guild of SS. Christopher and George in the area of St. George's Chapel on St. George's Day, 23 April.[151] The play, for which the waits provided a musical prologue, included the characters of St. George in armor (played by John Stamper, a tiler, in 1554[152]), the "king and Quene," their daughter ("the may," elsewhere known as Cleodolina), and a dragon, which not surprisingly needed mending.[153] The scene that was presented would have been the one that is extremely familiar from examples in the visual arts, including numerous fifteenth- and sixteenth-century examples in

York.[154] St. George, implored by a princess who has been chosen by lot to be sacrificed to the dragon, sets out to slay the pest and to make the country, ruled by the parents of the princess, free. Once the dragon is pierced with the lance, it is tamed and can be led with the girdle of the princess without danger. After the king and the people agree to be baptized, St. George kills the dragon.

One representation dated c.1530 in painted glass in St. Michael-le-Belfrey, York, shows St. George in plate armor with visor up and sword raised to slay the dragon below his feet.[155] The king, queen, and maiden are shown in a wood-carving on a chest now in the York Minster Chapter House. This carving illustrates the princess begging for help from St. George while her parents appear in separate windows in a walled city, whereupon St. George thrusts his lance through the dragon's mouth, and finally the princess leads the dragon with the girdle.[156] Less illustrative of the narrative are the illumination in the Bolton Hours (fol. 33^v), which shows the princess and her parents looking on during the conflict, and a fifteenth-century added drawing, associated with the painted glass of All Saints, North Street, York, in a psalter in the Bodleian Library (MS. Don.d.85, fols. 129^v-130). The latter also includes a lamb on a cord held by the princess, who is awaiting the outcome of the battle.[157]

Local devotion to a saint, often associated with local possession of relics, sometimes helped to inspire play production honoring the saint. At Coventry, however, where St. George was especially venerated (he was, after all, reputed to have been born in the county of Warwickshire[158]) and where the Cathedral of St. Mary possessed a significant relic identified in an inventory as "An Image of Saynt George with a bone of his in his shelde Syluer,"[159] a St. George's Day procession was apparently mounted under the auspices of the Shearmen and Tailors who had chosen this saint as their patron,[160] though there is no evidence of a play included in these festivities. Nevertheless, for royal entries in 1474 and 1498 St. George appeared as a participant, in both instances at the conduit in Cross Cheaping.[161] These appearances do not qualify as saint plays, of course, but the description of the action in the tableau in 1474 requires notice since it remarks on the presence of "seint George Armed and a kinges doughter knelyng a fore hym with a lambe and the fader and the moder beyng in a toure a boven beholdyng seint George savyng theire doughter from the dragon."[162] The conduit ran wine, organs played, and the saint spoke a short speech commenting on God's gift of the realm to the protection of Mary and himself "perpetuall/ hit to defende from enimies ffere and nere"; as the maiden was defended from the dragon, so may this prince be protected forever.[163] The account of 1498 also implies some minimal action of "seynt George kyllyng the dragon" and making a speech, which announces him as patron saint of the royal visitor, in this case Prince Arthur.[164]

St. George was, after all, the patron saint of England who had indeed displaced St. Edward the Confessor by the fourteenth century as the royal and national protector. Devotion to his cult was especially strong from the time of English involvement in the Third Crusade under Richard I.[165] An important event in the establishment of St. George as a saint of this rank was, of course, the founding of the Order of the Garter in c.1347.[166] The Order of the Garter had chosen St. George as its patron and regularly celebrated the feast of the saint; additionally, the order expressed its devotion to the saint through the famous iconography of St. George's Chapel at Windsor.[167] Henry V's devotion to the saint, culminating on St. Crispin's Day at Agincourt, will be remembered best surely through Shakespeare's ringing words "God for Harry, England, and Saint George!" (*Henry V* III.i.34). The Constitution of Archbishop Henry Chichele in 1415 declared St. George's Day to be a principal feast.[168] In 1504-05, Henry VII even obtained a relic of the saint, a leg, which in his will he bequeathed to the altar in his mortuary chapel.[169] As an exemplar of chivalry, St. George remained popular in England long after the Reformation, as the the presence of the Red Crosse Knight in the *Faerie Queene* of Edmund Spenser demonstrates. It is very clear that processions, ridings, and, when they occurred, plays functioned to promote social cohesiveness in ways that have come under scrutiny by scholars utilizing methodology recently pioneered by anthropologists, while at the same time social distinctions and rank were reinforced.[170]

A pageant of St. George at Ipswich was reported to have been presented at Corpus Christi between c.1400 and c.1542.[171] It might be tempting to believe that here we have something more than *tableaux vivants* in procession, and the existence of a book of Corpus Christi which needed mending in 1492 may seem at first to suggest something more dramatic. In 1504, the Corpus Christi feast is said to have a play, while in 1515 we read that the play of Corpus Christi will not be played for that year ("Et ludus vocatus Corpus Cristi pley pro hoc anno non luditur").[172] The last appearance in the civic records gives the order of the pageants, beginning with St. George in the place of precedence.[173] Unfortunately, John Wasson has demonstrated convincingly that there was no connection between the processional pageants and the plays at Ipswich.[174]

Likewise hard to interpret are the records of the St. George Riding at Norwich,[175] apparently dating from St. George's Day in 1408 and continuing to the Reformation, with remnants retained in civic practice into modern times. Snap the Dragon, which had been newly re-made in the early nineteenth century before the debased civic ceremonies were stopped by legislation prohibiting the procession in 1835, still exists.[176] The Riding was sponsored by the Guild of St. George founded in 1385 which also maintained an image of the saint in the Cathedral and required its members to participate in the services on the feast day of the saint.[177] The ordinances of the guild indicate that one of their number is yearly to be chosen to be George in the Riding and another to be his sword bearer to go before him, while others are to carry candles and a banner.[178]

An inventory of the goods of the guild in 1441-42 includes not only a relic of St. George—an arm, given by Sir John Fastolf and kept in the cathedral—borne by a silver and gilt angel,[179] but also other devices and images which testify to devotion to the saint. The seal of the guild, as a later inventory of 1469 explains, was "grauen' with an Image of Seynt George," and there were banners with his image and his coat of arms. Additionally there were other items associated with the Riding which, though probably not actually dramatic, might, for example, throw light on the costuming of St. George as well as other aspects of production in the plays dramatizing the life of this saint elsewhere in England:

> Item j gowne of scarlet for the George with blow garteryz lyned with grenetartaryn'.

> Item . . . a chapelet for the George with an Owche of Copre guylt with the armes of Seynt George in the myddes ij white gownes for the heynsmen'. . . .

> Item viij torches a dragon' j basnet j peyre gloues of plate a swerd with a pomel and hiltez of laton' a Scabard with boces of laton' couered with velwet j gowne Russet. . . .[180]

An inventory of 21 April 1550 indicates that a number of items were sold, including the following:

> Item a cote armour of white dammaske with a redde cros

> Item a Iackette of fustyan with a redde crosse

> Item a horse harnes of blak veluet with bokylles of copper & gilte, and a bytte to the same lente to the George

> Item a horse harneis of redde veluet with barres of copper and gylte, with out a bytte, with a fether therto for a george

> Item a horse harnes for the lady of Crymesen veluet and fflowers of golde without a bytte

> Item vj skutchens with St Georges crosse. . . .

> Item a Draggonne[181]

Among the other items in the inventory were numerous costumes, pieces of armor, banners, service books, a bell, and vestments. The "lady" in this list is St. Margaret, another character who overcame a dragon and likewise a saint pop-

64

ular in England. The Riding was revived under Queen Mary. However, in 1559 the Riding was prohibited: "Ther shalbe neyther George nor Margett But for pastyme the dragon to com In and shew hym selff as in other yeares."[182]

St. George plays were, however, reported in other locations. A Mayors List from Chester gives the date of 1430-31 and indicates that "in this yeare was St georges playes playd in chester."[183] At Lydd, in Kent, a "play of seint George" was reported to have been played before the Lieutenant of the Castle of Dover and his wife on 4 July 1455-56.[184] Payments for the preparation of "georges harnes" in 1531-32 and for the same task in 1532-33 indicate the saint's role there in a newly written play (either a new or revised text, or merely a newly copied text from the old book) prepared in 1526-27— "Itm' payde for a new Booke for the lyfe of Saynt George."[185] References to an "olde play boke" that was given or lent to a Mr. Gybson of London may provide some evidence for the suggestion that the old St. George playbook from Lydd became the basis for a play of St. George instituted at New Romney. In any case, Gybson's name appears in the New Romney records as somehow involved with a play at that town in 1532-33.[186] At Morebath, Devon, expense accounts in 1540 indicate the construction of a "city in the churchyard," apparently trestle staging with a rather elaborate set for a St. George play.[187]

It is less certain, however, that the St. George pageant at Dublin on St. George's Day c.1498 as reported in the Chain Book of Dublin was actually a fully staged drama,[188] though martyrdoms of saints were said to have been played there at Christmastime in 1528. In any case, for the St. George scene, whether *tableau vivant* or fully staged play, we again have evidence of guild involvement, with the Guild of St. George (which would have excluded the Irish from its membership in favor of persons of English descent) bearing the cost of paying the actors. These included "the Emperour and Empress with their followers, well apparelled, that is to say, the Emperor, with two Doctors, and the Empress, with two knights, and two maydens to beare the traynes of their gownes, well apparelled. . . ."[189] The actor playing St. George on horseback was to be paid 3s 4d by the Guild of St. George for the day. He was to be provided with four attendant horsemen-trumpeters on horses with a banner, "the pole-axe," and the swords of the Emperor and the warrior saint, these also to be paid by the guild. The dragon was to be led by "a mayd well aparelled" enlisted through the efforts of the "elder master of the yeald," while "a good line for the dragon" was to be provided by the Clerk of the Market.[190] Obviously, if the original event involved a play rather than merely a riding, it nevertheless would have focused on only one scene, the rescue of the princess from the dragon, which thereupon would probably have been led in procession through the city.

Full dramatic presentation of the St. George story is, however, indicated in the records from Bassingbourn, Cambridgeshire. Churchwardens' accounts from Bassingbourn for 1511 report a parish-sponsored theatrical on the subject of the "holy martir seynt georg" on the feast of St. Margaret, i.e., 20 July.[191] Money was collected from twenty-seven nearby villages for the play in addition to individual subscribers who gave gifts in kind, and expenses are itemized. The "garnement man" was paid 25s 2d for "garnements and propyrtes and play books," while minstrels and waits, the latter from Cambridge, were given 5s 6d for playing on three days, Wednesday, Sunday, and Monday. Payments were made for the making and painting of three falchions and four axes, the latter to be used by tormentors. There was the cost further of outfitting the dragon and the "car."[192] Quite interestingly, the drama seems to have been an elaborate one, with the martyrdom of the saint being an important aspect of the action. It is, however, unlikely that the normal scene of the rescue of the maiden would have been neglected, for a decade later the churchwardens' accounts of the same parish note the purchase of an image of St. George, which was made by a carver at Walden who also was to include "the kyng and the qwene."[193]

Representations of the martyrdom or other scenes from

St. George's life are, however, rare. Very early wall paintings (c.1135) at Hardham, Sussex, do show the events leading up to his death. Here the subjection of the dragon is followed by the saint before the the prefect, Dacian, who orders him to be tortured. He is hung by his hands, is imprisoned and perhaps tortured on the rack, and is bound to a wheel (which breaks). The final scenes are faded and indecipherable.[194] In woodcarving, there is of course the elaborate series on the stalls of St. George's Chapel, Windsor, where further scenes by medieval carvers show the nude saint first tied onto a hurdle and drawn by horses and then, in armor, placed on a board, where he is threatened and tortured by several men. He is also raised from the dead by the Virgin, tested with poison offered to him by a magician, Athanaise, as in the *Golden Legend* (fig. 17); stripped and placed onto the board (his legs and forearms have been amputated, while a man is cooking one of his hands in a pot over a fire); and, on desk fronts, kneeling and receiving his helmet from the Virgin and again being tortured on a hurdle dragged by horses.[195]

In painted glass, St. George's martyrdom is told uniquely in a late fifteenth-century window at St. Neot in Cornwall.[196] Though given an unfortunate "restoration" in 1830, the glass nevertheless illustrates some scenes which are not elsewhere presented in painted glass or other media in England. The glass shows him being raised from the dead by the Virgin following his participation in a battle with the "Gauls" and his death at their hands, whereupon he receives his helmet and other armor from her and attendant angels (fig. 10). Rushforth notes that this scene recalls "the ceremonial investiture and arming of a medieval knight at his creation."[197] Unfortunately, the scene is reported to be largely a restoration by Hedgeland, though enough was present in the original fragmentary panel to verify the basic iconography. The inscription reads: *Hic beata Maria armat Georgium.*[198] The saint is throughout recognized through the red cross emblem which he wears. A fifth scene illustrates the saint's battle with the dragon, during which the princess kneels as she watches the outcome from a nearby hill. St. George is then apprehended for refusing to worship idols and brought before Dacian; the inscription reads: *Hic capitur et ducitur ante regem.* Six tortures follow: (1) his body is torn with rakes, (2) he is hung from a gibbet (a millstone is attached to his feet, but this may be an addition of the restorer, and indeed the entire panel is labelled by Rushforth as "suspicious"), (3) he is thrown into a cauldron filled with molten lead (a spurious monk has been added by Hedgeland), (4) he is dragged by a horse (St. George is modern, but according to Rushforth the original "cannot have been very different from what we now see"[199]), (5) he is made to get down on his hands and knees and is ridden by the son of the Emperor, and (6) he is about to be beheaded as he kneels in his armor before an executioner.[200] The series, to be sure, differs somewhat from any published text of the St. George legend (the "riding" of the saint by the son of the Emperor is, for example, unique), but nevertheless will suggest some of the complexities that a fully staged play on the subject of this figure could draw upon.

The general narrative implied by the painted glass at St. Neot is additionally corroborated by alabaster retables of English origin, which, however, tend to simplify the story. A St. George retable (dated c.1460-1500) at La Celle, Normandy, for example, has the resurrection of the saint, his arming by the Virgin, his battle with the dragon, the baptism of the princess and her family, his appearance before Dacian, and his beheading.[201] Many of these scenes also appear on an alabaster at Borbjerg, Jutland, in Denmark, where two additional scenes show St. George drinking from the poisoned cup given to him by the magician and the saint kneeling before the temple of Apollo, represented by an idol in the shape of a devil with horns.[202] Close observation of the details illustrated in the alabasters, as in the painted glass, provides considerable additional detail relevant to the plays presented in medieval England—e.g., in the arming of St. George at Borbjerg, the saint, wearing contemporary plate armor, has his helmet placed over his head by the Virgin before whom he kneels, while an angel places the spurs on his feet. Two additional angels hold his lance and sword, while his horse appears in the background.[203] It is not possible, of course, to know precisely which scenes would have been dramatized, but careful observation of the iconographic programs chosen for the most popular contemporary forms, such as alabasters, are helpful in establishing what the probable episodes were.

VII

In addition to the lost dramas discussed above, British saint plays which have disappeared include the texts of a miracle play of St. Nicholas, most likely at Gloucester, in December 1283 and another possible play on this saint at the Scottish court in 1473;[204] a play of Mary Magdalene written by John Burgess at Magdalen College, Oxford, in 1506-07;[205] a play of St. John (described as "*Spectacula*") at London in 1508;[206] a play of SS. Feliciana and Sabina at Shrewsbury in 1516;[207] a three-day play of St. Christina reportedly indicated in a copy of the churchwardens' accounts at Bethersden, Kent, in 1522;[208] a "play of holy John of bowre" (St. John of Beverley?) at Grimsby, Lincolnshire, on 18 June 1527, and another of St. Martin at Colchester in the same year;[209] a pageant of St. Ursula, which perhaps involved dramatization, presented along with the pageant of St. Catherine by the London Drapers for the visit of the Danish king at Midsummer 1523 (possibly repeated in 1529);[210] and further pageants at London on the topics of St. Blythe (1512), St. John the Evangelist (1521, 1529), St. Margaret (1541),[211] and St. John the Baptist, which Machyn glowingy reported on 29 October 1553 as having "goodly speches."[212] This list, of course, can hardly make any claim to completeness.[213]

From the above list, the London Ursula pageant is particularly interesting because, as possibly (but hardly inevitably) in the case of the pageant for Catherine of Aragon, the records here definitely indicate a girl actress—the "eldest daughter" of one Childe—as well as "vj virgens" who were her constant companions.[214] Children played angels and other roles in the dramatization of the story of St. Margaret, and those who played angels were provided with garments of crimson silk. Richard Matthew, a skinner, played the "Sowden" in this pageant, which also included a dragon provided with a gallon of "aqua vyte" to produce flames from its mouth. Payment was also made to the person who "kept fire in the dragon's mouth."[215]

Lacking from our discussion thus far, of course, has been the matter of lost plays on the Miracles of the Virgin Mary. That such plays were part of the repertoire is indicated not only by a play of St. Mary recorded at New Romney, Kent, in 1512-13, but also by the two apparent fragments that we have of medieval saint plays, the only remnants in existence in addition to the complete plays—Cornish *St. Meriasek* and the two Digby plays on the subjects of the *Conversion of St. Paul* and *Mary Magdalene*. These fragments are one entitled *Dux Moraud* from the character whose speeches it contains, and another known as the *Durham Prologue,* both of which are printed in Norman Davis' edition of *Non-Cycle Plays and Fragments.*[216] *Dux Moraud* was a play about incest, murder, and guilt that has all the marks of a Miracle of the Virgin,[217] which would have culminated in the conversion and salvation of the villainous daughter.

The *Durham Prologue,* contained on a single sheet of parchment now in the Durham Cathedral Library, has recently been given close study by Stephen K. Wright,[218] who demonstrates how this fragment may be the introduction to a play on the topic of a miracle of the Virgin, specifically dramatizing the story of "The Knight Who Denied Christ but Not the Virgin." This tale sensationally tells of a profligate and pleasure-loving knight who impoverishes himself and then tries to raise more money by striking an agreement with the devil. The young knight, however, is also asked to deny the Virgin Mary, something he will not do. Ultimately his devotion to St. Mary saves him and provides for the forgiveness of his sin, for she intercedes for him. The knight then, through a fortunate marriage, is further able to regain all his wealth.[219]

It is certainly a pity that we do not possess further remnants of the Marian saint plays of the medieval period, especially since devotion to her cult was far more important than that extended to any other saint. Relics of the Virgin, often brought back to England by the crusaders and including such items as her "mylk in Syluer and gylt"[220] and fragments of her tomb or clothing,[221] were widely preserved. Plays on the subjects of her parentage, early life, death, funeral, assumption, and coronation as queen of heaven were included in great mystery cycles, of course,[222] and there is simply every reason to believe that plays on her miracles would have been part of the standard repertoire of the medieval stage in Britain as it was on the continent.[223]

VIII

The two extant saint plays in Middle English are both contained in Digby MS. 133 in the Bodleian Library, Oxford.[224] The play of *Mary Magdalene,* contained in folios 95-145 of the manuscript, is a long drama on the subject of a feminine saint who was ranked in the Middle Ages as one of the apostles; in the play, she gives testimony to her presence at Pentecost where she was included in the gift of tongues and the ability "to vndyrstond every langwage" (ll. 1343-44). She is an important figure in English art,[225] and her person was closely associated with the idea of the Church itself. As such, she was seen as an exemplar of the Christian life in its ideal form, providing a pattern for all to follow in movement from a fallen state to penitence and then to carefully introspective contemplation.

The Mary Magdalene of the drama and of her legend was much more than merely a biblical saint, since her life is extended to include episodes that are said to have occurred after the events told in the Bible. The play, which is highly episodic, treats a long expanse of time, reaching from the events prior to her fall and conversion and extending up to the point of her death far away from Jerusalem in Provence. Some critics have nevertheless pointed to certain elements of unity that bind together the diverse scenes.[226] It is, in any case, a comprehensive play in its presentation of those visual tableaux which are important from the standpoint of devotion to the saint, while it further adds, sometimes in an imaginative way, additional characters and tableaux to fill out the story and even simply to entertain the audience. Thus is the play designed to move from *exempla* of pride to the representation of humility and faith, which in turn are able to achieve miraculous results in keeping with the transcendental power that flows through this saint.

The cult of Mary Magdalene was, of course, particularly significant in the later Middle Ages, though English devotion to this saint has been traced back to Anglo-Saxon times.[227] In England, more than 170 pre-Reformation church dedications to her are recorded,[228] and her relics appear to have been particularly valued. Exeter Cathedral very early had a finger of the Magdalen, for example, and Eleanor of Aquitaine is said to have offered some hair of Mary Magdalene at the Shrine of Edward the Confessor.[229] There is an amazing story of St. Hugh of Lincoln who, visiting Fécamp, was shown the arm of the Magdalen in cloth wrapping, which to the horror of the monks of the abbey he slashed open with a knife; then he attempted to break away a piece, finally biting off a portion of a finger with his teeth and handing it to his attendant with the intention of taking this relic with him to England.[230]

Great impetus had been given to the cult by the discovery of her relics at Vezeley in the eleventh century.[231] Osbern Bokenham reports in his *Legendys of Hooly Wummen* that after her burial in Provence by St. Maximin, the body of "Thys holy apostelesse, Marye Mawdelyn," was a "long tym aftyr," in 749 A.D., "Translatyd from this seyd place . . . to vizelyac, and ther leyd in shryne/ By oon clepyd Gyrard, a lord in burgundye,/ Wher as men wene she yet doth lye."[232] But she was widely available through the broader dispersion of her relics and through the common presence of her image in parish churches and chapels in England. As a saint now crowned "in blysse in the heuenly regyoun," she is, according to Bokenham, in a position to guide and give governance to all her "seruauntys in erthe" and to keep them always under her protection (ll. 6305-08).

The Digby play presents a heroine who, following the Western medieval tradition, is a conflation of several persons in the biblical account—i.e., the penitent woman who comes to wash and anoint Jesus' feet at the house of Simon, the sinful woman from whom Christ casts out seven devils, and, finally, the sister of Lazarus and Martha. This traditional Mary Magdalene has been called the "single Magdalene," and represents an understanding of her character that dates back at least to St. Gregory the Great.[233] The single Magdalene hence is to be found in the liturgy as well as in her widely known legend as it was retold in the *Golden Legend* and other collections of saints' lives.[234] Challenge to the Western tradition eventually came in 1518, when Jacques Lefèvre d'Etaples, a humanist, raised his voice in arguments against identifying the various persons that had been conflated in the usual understanding of Mary Magdalene.[235] Nevertheless, even at this date, the single Magdalene had defenders—e.g., St. John Fisher, who insisted that "no one must be given credence against the long accepted as well as deeply confirmed usage of the Church unless he produces invincible testimony from Scriptures or an absolutely unanswerable reason."[236] Those who would deny the single Magdalene were, Fisher complained, intent upon removing a lesser light from the heavens and allowing only the greater, the Blessed Virgin.[237] For the medieval Church, it was indeed important to connect repentance, devotion, and contemplation, which were regarded as three aspects of the ideal life of faith to be followed to whatever extent possible by all who would achieve salvation and ultimate life with God.

The portion of the Digby manuscript which contains the play of *Mary Magdalene* has been dated by Donald C. Baker, John L. Murphy, and Louis B. Hall on the basis of the watermark found in the paper, which suggests a date of c.1515-25.[238] The manuscript, however, represents a copy of the original text: lines (and, at one point, a whole page) are missing; speeches are confused and even, in one case, repeated; and on the whole the job is not well done—indeed, so ill done that at the bottom of fol. 129 the scribe in his frustration has exclaimed "Jhesu mercy."[239] A reference to "ten poundys of nobyllys cler" (l. 1920) has suggested to the play's most recent editors that a pre-1500 date may be indicated by this numismatic evidence, for in the sixteenth century it was more usual to use the term 'noble' as a designation of an amount of money rather than with reference to a coin.[240] For the dating of the play itself, then, we can only assume that it was written some years prior to the copy which appears in the manuscript—i.e., that the play dates from the late fifteenth century—and that it was the work of an author working in East Anglia, which provided the dialect utilized in the drama.

While Jacob Bennett has insisted that the linguistic evidence would localize the play at King's Lynn,[241] there is nothing in the dramatic records of this municipality to suggest production of the play there. No guild there is dedicated to Mary Magdalene, for example, and no dramatic records from King's Lynn suggest performance of a drama such as the *Mary Magdalene*. We do know that there was a guild devoted to Mary Magdalene in the late Middle Ages at Wiggenhall,[242] where this saint is also included among others extant on the painted screen in the church; in this example, she is shown with long hair and holding her traditional ointment jar in her left hand (fig. 11). A much more likely location would, however, be Norwich, where at least as early as 1286 there was an annual fair on the Magdalen's feast day, 22 July,[243] a date which would obviously be quite favorable for a lavish outdoor production of a play of the type represented by *Mary Magdalene*. The procession on this day is noted in the Norwich records, which indicate that it was reinstated in 1533 though suppressed in 1538.[244] The procession started at the Mayor's Gate by 1 p.m., with the mayor, sheriffs, aldermen, and "before them the watche in harnes" riding to the fair as formerly, since "of late the . . . auncient and laudable custome hath been discontynewid," and doing

their "devocion wythynne the chapell of Saynt Marye Magdalen there"; thereafter all would spend their "tyme in the
wreslyng Place, atte the cost and charge of the said Mayer."[245]
The "wresling place" was certainly a kind of location utilized
for the showing of sports and perhaps other shows, even
potentially including plays. It here is not therefore impossible
that the fair might have included the staging of the play of
Mary Magdalene using more or less the text as we now have
it in the Digby manuscript.

John Coldewey has suggested further that the play of
Mary Magdalene, along with the *Conversion of St. Paul* also
contained in the same manuscript, might have been produced
at Chelmsford, Essex, in the summer of 1562, thus explaining
how the manuscripts of these two plays found themselves
into the hands of Miles Blomefield of that town.[246] Coldewey's arguments are circumstantial with regard to the
question of the revival of *Mary Magdalene* at Chelmsford so
long after the establishment of Elizabeth I as queen of England, though the use of what would on the surface seem to
be the story of a biblical saint might have been tolerated
prior to 1570. Nevertheless, the Digby *Mary Magdalene* is
extremely closely linked with the pre-Reformation Magdalen
cult and with the iconography associated with this saint prior
to the iconoclasm which accompanied the Reformation in
England. Queen Elizabeth's Royal Injunctions of 1559 were
explicit in their insistence on the "abolishment of things su-
perstitious," demanding "that they shall take away, utterly
extinct and destroy all shrines, coverings of shrines, all tables,
candlesticks, trindals, and rolls of wax, pictures, paintings,
and all other monuments of feigned miracles, pilgrimages,
idolatry and superstition, so that there remain no memory
of the same in walls, glasses, windows, or elsewhere within
their churches and houses. . . ."[247] There was no encouragement given to the cults of the saints, not even of an
"apostelesse" such as Mary Magdalene, in the Protestant
climate under Elizabeth.

The presentation of the Digby play, as we might expect
in the case of an East Anglian drama, almost certainly uti-

lized place-and-scaffold staging rather than pageant wagon or processional staging. Perhaps Magdalene Castle was placed centrally in the playing area, a feature that links it with *The Castle of Perseverance*.[248] Reference to continental examples, especially the Lucerne plans for the production in the Weinmarkt Square in 1583,[249] will provide some sensible suggestions concerning the arrangement of the acting area in early productions of the *Mary Magdalene,* with mansions representing various locations distributed at convenient distances from each other. Such an arrangement would be more practical in its use of space than the circular stage plans put forward by Albright and Bevington, though Bevington is undoubtedly correct to see some of the scaffolds as oriented according to the symbolic meanings assigned to East (the direction toward which we would expect to look toward God's scaffold, since in churches the East end is the portion of the church devoted to chancel and high altar), or North (associated with the devil).[250] Minor structures, such as Mary Magdalene's arbor, the lodge at the gate of the palace at Marcylle, or the rock where the Queen of Marcylle is left behind, may well, as Richard Beadle has suggested, have been put up and taken down as the play progressed.[251] There thus were theatrical affinities with the Creation to Doom cycles, particularly with N-town, which likewise is now commonly believed to be East Anglian in origin, and also with the morality plays of East Anglia, including specifically, of course, *The Castle of Perseverance.* Historical, legendary, and realistic characters appear on the stage along with allegorical ones in what might be described as a typically late-medieval mixture of dramatic modes. We see such a mixture often in contemporary art, however, and hence the inclusion of allegory can hardly be called an "intrusion" into the drama.[252] If the diabolic trinity—i.e., the three enemies of man who are the World, the Flesh, and the Devil, which are always rejected in the rite of baptism—appears with the Seven Deadly Sins who make their appearance in a manner which may remind us of the Macro moralities, it is nevertheless needful to remember that these figures are actually necessary in the narrative of the single Magdalene.

In *Luke* 8.2, "seven devils" are said to have been driven out of "Mary who is called Magdalen" (Douay). These seven demons are, according to Gregory the Great, the Seven Deadly Sins.[253] The idea is picked up in vernacular literature, as illustrated by *Jacob's Well*:

> as Marye mawdelen dede, wassche thou the feet of crist, that is, his manhod, wyth wepyng terys in thi confessioun, and crist schal cacche out of the vij. feendys, that is, vij. dedly synnes, as he dede out of marye mawdelen. and thanne schalt thou haue forȝeuenesse and mercy, as sche hadde and seynt Petyr for here wepyng.[254]

Hence when the scene calls for the expulsion of seven demons out of the penitent woman, the Seven Deadly Sins are called upon to be *"conveyyd into the howse of Symont Leprovs"* where, changing their garments so that they will be *"arayyd lyke seuen dylf"* (l. 563sd), they will remain until they receive their cue, which will be Christ's absolution of the sinful woman followed by his command to depart in peace: *"Vade in pace"* (l. 691). Then they *"xall dewoyde from the woman,"* whereupon they will return, along with the Bad Angel, *"into hell wyth thondyr,"* presumably entering the nether region through a traditional hell mouth.

The effect involved in having the Seven Deadly Sins *"dewoyde from the woman"* may be visualized through comparison with scenes in the *Holkham Bible Picture Book* in which Christ on several occasions causes an ugly and hairy devil to leave the body of a suffering individual. On folios 23, 23ᵛ, 24, and 25ᵛ Jesus causes hairy, horned devils with batlike wings and claw feet to come forth from the mouths of those whom he heals and absolves. In an Italian example actually showing Mary Magdalene anointing Christ's feet during the meal at Simon's house, a wall painting by Giovanni da Milano of c. 1365 at the Church of San Croce, Florence, the seven devils are escaping through the roof.[255] The idea that the sins exit from the woman's mouth, however, would seem to be an effect entirely dependent upon the available technology, which may have been too clumsy to make this work.

Prior to their assault on Mary Magdalene, the Seven Deadly Sins are divided into three categories, each of which is placed under the control of one of the members of the diabolic trinity—i.e., as noted above, the World, the Flesh, and the Devil.[256] Pride and Covetousness attend the World, who, seated in state surely with all the symbols of earthly power, brags that "the whele of fortune with me hath sett his senture" and that "In me restyt the ordor of the metellys seuyn" which in turn are associated with the planets and, presumably, with the ordering of the cosmos (ll. 312ff). The first of these claims is correct, for, in contrast to the wheel of life which has the deity at its center,[257] Fortune's unstable wheel indeed does have the world as its focus, since those who would rise in worldly power and fame must have secular ambitions rather than spiritual hope. Nevertheless, the second claim is a gross overstatement, for it suggests a level of authority that has actually not been given to the World, whose reign must be over the sub-lunar sphere.[258] While Pride may salute the World as the source of all happiness for humans who are living under his dominion, the latter nevertheless is the personification of all that is giddy and unstable—i.e., subject to the vicissitudes of fortune (personified, of course, as Fortuna). The World, in other words, has something in common with Giotto's Inconstancy, struggling to retain her balance on a wheel, in the Arena Chapel at Padua.[259]

The World further represents precisely the kind of fraudulent claims to dominion which have already been set forth in the play of *Mary Magdalene* by Caesar, Herod, and Pilate. The values implied by the World therefore represent one category to be rejected by any saint, whose trust must be placed in a transcendent power more stable than this inconstant figure.

If a degree of caricature is suggested in the play by the figure of the World, the presentation of the King of Flesh and his cohorts—his "fayere spowse Lechery," his knight

78

Gluttony, and Sloth—indicates even more broad use of this device of characterization which is designed further to undercut the credibility of these figures.[260] On stage, these allegorical characters may have had some affinity with the graphic representations of Luxuria, Gula, and Desidia in the engravings illustrating the Seven Deadly Sins formerly attributed to Brueghel, though the latter are from the continent and somewhat later in date than the play.[261] The drama shows Flesh embracing and kissing Lechery, mirroring the standard iconographic representation of *luxuria*: a pair of lovers embracing, as in the lost wall painting at Ingatestone,[262] and also often fondling each other.[263] Very significantly, once Lechery has successfully tempted Mary to fall, she will then shortly appear in the embraces of her lover, Curiosity. After she has turned from the sins of the flesh, she devotes herself first to true works of love, and at the end of her life to the rejection of all *gula* and *accidia* to such an extent that she will give up all earthly food in her total dedication to the things of the spirit.

Wrath and Envy are the Devil's retainers, and his stage is appropriately located immediately over the hell mouth. The warfare of the vices against "Mannis sowle" is, of course, initiated by the Devil, whose motives are clearly his own wrath and envy directed against that which is potentially good but also against the source of all good. His goal is the ruin of souls, which also implies his own ruin. In a wall painting of c. 1400 formerly at Brooke Church in Norfolk, the standing figure of Wrath stabbed himself in the chest with knives as he looked to the left, the direction that is associated with damnation rather than salvation; below him was the mouth of hell, which was swallowing him up.[264] Traditionally, Envy eats its own heart in a similarly self-destructive act.[265] Not only these but also the other forces of evil are under the Devil's command in the siege of Mary Magdalene's castle.

The castle is a familiar scenic unit utilized by the late medieval stage as well as a standard detail in iconography.[266] The appearance of the castle in the play is not arbitrary for another reason, however. The Vulgate uses the word *castel-*

lum to translate the Greek word *koma* which signifies 'village' in *Luke* 10.38-39, the passage that describes how Jesus "entered into a certain town [*castellum*]: and a certain woman named Martha, received him into her house. And she had a sister called Mary, who sitting also at the Lord's feet, heard his word" (Douay). Mirk's *Festial,* for example, refers to "Mary Mawdelen" of "Mawdelen-castell," while Bokenham further explains that this castle was inherited by the Magdalen from her father "Syre" "Wher-of she namyd was Magdalyne" (ll. 5383-86).[267] As pilgrims to Jerusalem had discovered, however, Bethany was indeed a fortified village with stone walls—a village included in the regular pilgrim itinerary because of the presence of the tomb of Lazarus in village's church.[268] In the drama the fortification, which Mary here also has inherited from her father, may instantly be recognized as the familiar Castle of Virtue intended to be seen as a sign of the defense which the soul adapts or builds for itself against vice. The allegory may bear comparison with the episode of Alma's castle in *The Faerie Queene*: the soul, who could only be perfectly safe in the event that the senses which are the gateways to the world were closed up, must constantly be on guard against the members of the diabolic trinity and/or their servants, the Seven Deadly Sins. Lady Lechery, however, does find entrance into Magdalene Castle, and Mary is tempted to give up mourning for her father, to surrender the "governans" of her castle, and to plunge herself into all the delights promised by a life of pleasure. She chooses cupidity, which gives priority to selfish enjoyment and which is contrary to the true life of love as taught in the traditional teachings of the Church.

For the modern critic who remains fixed in modern notions about causation and motivation, Mary's easy descent into vice must seem dramatically and theatrically implausible. Hence Robert H. Bowers finds the scene of her seduction to be "an artistic failure."[269] The "characters are never fully realized," he complains, and thus "We are reading narration, or 'closet-drama,' rather than authentic drama. In addition, one feels that the aureate language and the postur-

ing of the main characters are almost calculated euphe-
misms, society devices employed by the author to keep vitality
at a safe distance far from the manor, and to avoid serious
consideration of the human condition."[270] Yet a potential
motive for the Magdalen's lapse must have been known to
the author of the Digby play. As Mirk reports, Mary was to
marry St. John, but God commanded him instead to remain
celibate, with the result that "Mary was wrath, and ʒaf her
al to synne and namely to lechery, un so moch that scho
lost the name of Mawdelen, and was callyd the synfull
woman."[271] In spite of promising material that could have
created a sensational scene in the play, therefore, the author
of the Digby *Mary Magdalene* instead follows a simpler pattern that is based on the *Golden Legend,* which indeed denies
the authenticity of the betrothal of the Magdalen to St.
John.[272] The *Golden Legend,* however, insists that

> for soo moche as she shone in bewte gretly and in richesse
> / so moche the more she submysed her body to delyte / And
> therfore she loste her right name, and was called customably
> a synner.[273]

Bokenham gives the same account of the loss of her name
and indicates that because of her ill fame she was known
simply as "Marie the synnere" (l. 5408).

It is very odd therefore that when Mary Magdalene cat-
alogues her sins at lines 682-84 she lists only "pryde" and
"wrath and envy," sins that to be sure are directly opposed
to the humility, patience, and charity which she cultivates
from the time of her conversion. The vices of pride, wrath,
and envy are prominent in the legend told by Mirk, but otherwise we might feel that of these only pride seems particularly
appropriate in a list of the sins of a prostitute. Curiously,
wrath and envy would have been exactly right if the playwright had retained the story of Mary's reaction to the breaking off of St. John's betrothal as we have it in Mirk's account.
In the end it is necessary to conclude that the action in the
play is more emblematic than realistic. Mary's fall from grace

81

is a willing act in response to the fraudulent but demonic enticements of evil. It is a fall that, however, is not depicted with view to the creation of so-called "fully developed" or "three dimensional" characters such as might be encountered in modern narrative.

Having surrendered herself to Lady Lechery, Mary Magdalene goes with her to the city, Jerusalem, where she participates in the service of infidelity—a service of eating and drinking which Theresa Coletti has identified as a "mock-Eucharistic feast."[274] Ironically, she calls the "wytty and wyse" taverner a "grom of blysse" (ll. 470, 489). The tavern setting is absolutely fitting, because here the Devil's minister will teach lessons which promote "glotonye" and "leccherye" as well as other sins.[275] Indeed, as the author of *Jacob's Well* insists, the tavern is not only the "scolehous" of the Devil but also his "chapel," where "his dyscyples stodyen and syngyn, bothe day and ny3t. . . ."[276] This is where the Devil performs his miracles, which are antithetic to those which God performs "in his chapel of holy cherche": the Devil makes men blind, takes from them their power to speak, and defrauds them of their rational powers.[277] The tavern especially encourages the repetition of man's earliest reputed *act* of sin, gluttony, which stimulates other appetites as well.[278] The demonic nature of gluttony is neatly represented in the wall painting formerly at Brooke, Norfolk, where Gluttony was shown with either vomit or demonic flames coming from his mouth, and also with flames rising from a wooden vessel beside him.[279] Mary, worshipping in the darkness of the Devil's church,[280] very quickly becomes guilty of the deadly sin of *luxuria,* which here is clearly related to the pleasures of eating and drinking.[281] The first stage is her willingness to sin, signified by her removal from the castle of virtue, and this is transformed in the second stage into action after Lady Lechery introduces her to the gallant, Curiosity, who is without question an insufferable upstart. He begins by appealing to Mary's pride when he praises her clothing, and then very rapidly thereafter makes a protestation of his love for her. Initially she seems to be shocked:

she protests that she is no whore. However, though he is not able to provide a convincing answer to her question concerning the cause of his sudden love, she nevertheless accepts his offer to dance.

The dance of Mary Magdalene to the music of transverse flute and drum is usefully illustrated in an engraving, dated 1519, by Lucas van Leyden (fig. 12) and sometimes called "The Worldly Pleasures of Mary Magdalene."[282] The dance, like the embrace, is commonly utilized to represent *luxuria,* as in miniatures in illustrated copies of Prudentius' *Psychomachia* (e.g., Cambridge, Corpus Christi College Library MS. 23, fol. 21ᵛ). In this manuscript, the vice Luxuria is vigorously dancing either with or before a young man to the accompaniment of a triple pipe and a lyre while two other young men stand behind him.[283] Additional proof illustrating Mary Magdalene as a dancer prior to her conversion has been found in the continental drama—e.g., in the Frankfurt Passion Play, where she exclaims that she wishes to dance to the pipe.[284] Even the type of dancing in which she supposedly engaged has been identified. Colin Slim has determined that in the later Middle Ages and Renaissance her dance was a basse dance.[285] When Mary Magdalene finishes dancing with her gallant, she surrenders herself to his will and ironically protests her absolute faithfulness to him (ll. 543-46). As the Devil and his followers rejoice over the soul that has fallen into their grasp, she exclaims over Curiosity's praiseworthy qualities.

Curiosity, as the Bad Angel suggests, is in actuality only a disguise that has been taken by Pride, and for Mary Magdalene pride is hence the Deadly Sin which inclines her to the activity associated with *luxuria.* Traditionally, of course, *superbia* is the root of all the other Deadly Sins:

> Seynt Gregory seyth in libro moralium, pryde . . . is rote and begynning of all synne and vicys, ffor ryght as ne wer this rote of a tre hyd onder the erde sal no braunche growyn owte ther of. Ryth soo ne qwer pride rotyd in mannys hert then sulde non braunches of synne spryngyn ther froo.[286]

83

Pride involves an attempt to assert one's self-sufficiency. Ultimately the proud person's principal concern is with himself or herself, a fact which is emblematically set forth in various representations of the Deadly Sin of Pride in the visual arts. Thus Pride in the wall painting formerly at Brooke Church, Norfolk, was a fashionably dressed young man who held a mirror in his right hand while he was combing his hair with his left, and the engraving attributed to Brueghel shows Superbia as an elaborately dressed woman who is admiring herself in a mirror, while the image in the mirror provides demonic mockery of her pretensions. [287] In continental plays, a mirror often actually appears as a stage property associated with the Magdalen,[288] whose focus is on her own body, its beauty, and the clothing and jewelry which adorn it rather than on more appropriate matters which ought to concern her. The initial sin of Lucifer was pride. In Eden, pride must likewise have been prior to the act of eating the forbidden fruit. So too is Mary Magdalene in the play caught in Pride's snare when she turns from her castle of virtue to move toward the city of Jerusalem where she will engage in the sports of that city. The other sins will follow in due course.

Nevertheless, though it is a species of pride, Curiosity or *Curiositas* has an independent existence in medieval iconography. In the sculpture that appears on the North Porch of Chartres Cathedral, *Curiositas* appears in the shape of an ape, an animal which symbolizes self-seeking pride and unrestrained indulgence in one's appetites.[289] The gallant Curiosity, the ape of fashion and surely a type despised by the East Anglian audience, thus precisely mirrors the Magdalen's spiritual state.[290] She is one who now is turned in upon herself and her pleasures. As a chanson, "Maugre danger pompera Magdalene," copied c.1510—a composition which may, according to Slim, have been connected with a play—indicates, she is beautiful, aristocratic, self-centered, passionate, and very promiscuous:

"De mon plaisir
Je suis seure et certaine

J'ay biens assez
En ung logis exquis;
Et mon gent corps si est
De maintes gens requis,
    Parquoy me dis
Sur toutes souveraine."

("I am sure and certain of my own pleasure; I have goods
enough in a charming lodging; and my beautiful body is much
in demand by many people; so I call myself sovereign over all
other women.")[291]

In the fourteenth-century *Queen Mary's Psalter,* Mary Magdalene is shown standing, accompanied by another woman, talking with three young men. Her left hand gestures with palm up and index finger extended. Rather untypically, she wears a veil and a long gown, as does the other woman, but both provocatively hold onto their gowns at the waist with their right hands. The man in front gestures in return. It is quite clearly a scene of immodest flirtation.[292]

After leaving with Curiosity to satisfy a hunger for something other than food and wine, Mary Magdalene is next seen in the play as she is waiting in an arbor, a fairly standard scenic device, where she will stay "Tyll som lovyr wol apere" (l. 570). She stresses her inconstancy by referring (in the plural) to her "valentynys" and her "lovys so dere" (ll. 564-65). There is no way in which we might discover precisely what costume was utilized in early performances in East Anglia, but surely she must have been dressed in garb indicative of her new occupation as a courtesan who caters to rich clients. The playwright was very aware of clothing and indeed, as Theresa Coletti indicates, makes of it a major motif that runs through the drama.[293] When Mary leaves her sinful life behind, she will also change to a different kind of clothing that reflects the humility which she has accepted as the antithesis of her previous pride. At the end of the drama, her clothing will be even further reduced, for traditionally at the conclusion of her life she neglected her garments totally while her long hair grew longer to cover her body and preserve her modesty—a natural garment perhaps most splendidly illustrated in the *Sforza Hours.*[294]

Mary's conversion comes, however, without preparation as she is lying among the fragrant flowers of the arbor. The change in her life is simply effected by the reproach of her Good Angel who chides her for her instability in a vision: "Why art thou aʒens God so veryabyll?" (l. 590). She is reminded to think of the God who "made the of nowth" and warned to "leve thi werkes wayn and veryabyll" (l. 590-91). A threat is added: if she persists in living a life of selfish pleasure and of pride, her "sowle xal lyyn in helle fyr" (ll. 596-97); therefore, the Good Angel warns, "Remembyr the on mercy, make thi sowle clyr" (l. 600). Awakening, she recognizes that she has "synnyd on euery syde" (l. 607) and resolves to "porsue the Prophett wherso he be,/ For he is the welle of perfyth charyte"; he also represents the "oyle of mercy" which shall "relyff" her (ll. 610-12).[295] There is a recognition here that she has previously acted absurdly and offensively against her "makar, of mytys most" (l. 632), and she herself knows that only the grace of Christ can now rescue her from her despair (ll. 634-35). Additionally, the play in its appeal to the audience thus underlines the cultic function of the saint in turning from despair to hope—a turning that is part of the regular pattern of Christian life but also an action in which the individual can be assisted by the saint herself, to whom he or she might petition for such help.

Normally the individual in the period immediately prior to the Reformation would appeal to the saint through her image, which would function as a window to the saint herself, utilizing prayers and wax candles to bridge the gap between the living individual and the saint whose soul is with God.[296] The most common way of representing the Magdalen in alabaster carvings, wall paintings, painted glass, etc., was with her emblem, the alabaster box of ointment which she traditionally carries.[297] So at line 613 in the play, Mary Magdalene resolves to seek Christ "Wyth swete bawmys," whereupon she sets forth with weeping and presumably appropriate gestures of lamentation to the house of Simon where she will wash *the fett of the prophet wyth the terrys of hur yys, whypyng hem with hur herre, and than anoynt hym wyth a precyus noyttment"* (l. 640*sd*). Her pilgrimage to see the prophet is shown in a panel of c.1475 by the Italian artist Carlo Crivelli which shows the penitent, carrying the jar of precious ointment before her, attired in her finery but with her carefully coiffured hair released so that it flows down her back.[298] (Her long blond hair,[299] which she calls attention to by holding a strand of it, is common in English iconography.) The next scene is, of course, very commonly illustrated in the visual arts in representations which range from the simple little woodcut in the Sarum Breviary printed at Paris in 1531 (fol. lxxxix) to the illustration in the *Holkham Bible Picture Book* (fol. 25ᵛ) or the the miniature in *Queen Mary's Psalter,* fol. 300. The latter typically shows her in front with her pot of ointment and anointing the feet of Christ, who is seated behind the table. She is literally lying on the floor, and her long hair is flowing out. On the table are food and drink, including two fish. The host is seated at the right of Christ, who is gesturing with two fingers extended to him. Two apostles are also at the table.[300]

In accord with the account in *Luke* 7.40-46, Jesus tells the parable of the two debtors while the penitent woman "wyth teres of hyr bettyr wepyng . . . wassheth [his] fete" and anoints them "wyth onymentys, lowly knelyng," and thereafter wipes them "wyth hur her, fayur and brygth shynnyng" (ll. 666-70). Mary Magdalene, whose previous life has been most dissolute, is now "most beholddyn" to him for healing her of the disease of deadly sin. Jesus speaks to her:

> Woman, in contryssyon thou art expert,
> And in thi sowle hast inward mythe,
> That sumtyme were in desert,
> And from therknesse hast porchasyd lyth.
> Thy feyth hath savyt the, and made the bryth! (ll. 686-90)

At the words *"Vade in pace"* (l. 691), the *"seuyn dyllys xall dewoyde frome the woman."* From darkness she has been rescued to become, according to Jacobus de Voragine, the light giver.[301] Quite appropriately thereafter at lines 768-75 when Mary is reunited with her brother and sister, she speaks a translation of the first nine lines of the popular devotional hymn *Christe qui lux es et dies* which praises Christ for being the light of the world and of all who follow him.[302] She who has been asleep in darkness, therefore, now participates in the iconography of light. From the standpoint of the early audience of this play she hence verifies the pattern of repentance, confession, and absolution which is capable of flooding the individual's soul with a similar light.

By the expulsion of the seven devils which are the Seven Deadly Sins from the Magdalen, Christ shows his power over Hell. In his raising of Lazarus from the grave, he shows his power over Death.[303] In these actions he asserts his authority to loose both souls and bodies from the forces of evil and hell—a power that is represented by the keys of the kingdom that are given by him to St. Peter as the representative of his newly-founded historical Church on earth. The two incidents also foreshadow the harrowing of hell (reported by a devil in lines 963-92) and Christ's own resurrection (reported by the angels in lines 1023-30). Furthermore, as an essential part of the play's devotional message, Christ in his incarnation brings eternal steadfastness into Time so that his followers may also overcome Hell and Death and thus achieve salvation.

The soteriological emphasis of Christ's ministry, crucifixion, and resurrection is particularly underlined in the *Hortulanus* scene, which was widely illustrated in the visual arts. In the *Peterborough Psalter* of the early fourteenth century, the Magdalen is kneeling with her hands raised and joined before a Christ who is holding a cross staff with his left hand and extending both his right hand and right foot with their wounds for her to see. The loose garment that he is wearing also displays the wound in his side, which is bleeding. The garden location is indicated only by a carefully pruned tree in the background.[304] A miniature in the *Gough Psalter* is similar in many respects, though there is less emphasis on the wounds and under Mary's veil her curls are showing.[305] In *Queen Mary's Psalter*, she extends her ointment jar toward him,[306] an iconographic detail that seems reflected in the Digby play when she offers to anoint him "wyth this bamys sote" (l. 1071). Her hair is, we should remember, her secondary emblem—e.g., she thus has long hair in a *Hortulanus* scene on a roof boss in the nave of Norwich Cathedral.[307] In late medieval painted glass in the East window at East Harling, Norfolk, the saint holds her jar with her left hand and her hair with her right hand as it has fallen over her shoulder and past her waist (fig. 14).[308] But the important innovation in the visual arts was to show Christ in a garden as a gardener holding a spade. The earliest example of this iconography may be in a Gospel Book of c.1230-39 from St. Chapelle (Paris, Bibliothèque Nationale MS. lat. 8892, fol. 12).[309] One of the two fourteenth-century cloister bosses that show *Hortulanus* scenes at Norwich Cathedral presents him in a gardener's hat and tunic with a knife in a sheath at his side and holding a spade.[310] An alabaster published by Dr. Hildburgh illustrates Christ holding his cross staff in his right hand and a spade in his left as Mary, with her jar in her left hand and a strand of her hair in her right hand, kneels before him. Another alabaster, in the Victoria and Albert Museum, depicts Christ in a gardener's hat and tunic, which he raises with his right hand, presumably to show his wounds in his feet.[311]

The spade is important from the standpoint of the iconography since it relates the risen Christ to the first Adam, who was forced to use a spade after the fall;[312] now that the fall is rectified by Christ as the second Adam, he appears holding this instrument upon his first meeting with one of his followers, Mary Magdalene, who was even regarded by some of the Church Fathers as a kind of second Eve.[313] In the Digby *Mary Magdalene,* Christ's allegorical explanation of his role as gardener thus takes on a new significance: "Mannys hartt is my gardyn here" and in it he sows "sedys of vertu all the ȝere" (ll. 1081-82). This point had been made with regard to Mary Magdalene long ago by Gregory the Great,[314] and Odo of Cluny further provides a gloss on the action at this point in the play:

> This woman was not entirely mistaken when she thought the
> Lord was a gardener. For just as the duty of a gardener is to
> eradicate harmful weeds so that good plants may be able to
> come forth, so the Lord Jesus daily eradicates vices from His
> garden, that is from His Church, so that virtue may increase.[315]

It is useful to contrast the difficulty with which Adam in the
Anglo-Norman *Adam* combats the thorns and thistles in their
field following the planting of wheat.[316] In contrast, as Christ
tells Mary Magdalene, "Whan that gardyn is watteryd wyth
terys clere,/ Than spryng vertuus, and smelle full sote" (ll.
1084-85).

For the garden of the soul to be tended successfully,
steadfastness in virtue is required, as Christ reminds Mary
prior to his disappearance. (He returns again, of course, to
give his blessing to the other faithful Marys, and thereafter
shows himself on the heaven stage above.) Mary Magdalene,
to whom Christ has lent his grace, is no longer the rebellious
and pleasure-loving woman, but the pattern of perfect penitence whose humility—a virtue which, after all, is the root
of all good[317]—establishes an appropriate model of behavior
for the whole Church. The staging of this play thus functioned on another level to reinforce social values regarded
as good and to promote virtues which were seen as sup-
porting social cohesiveness as opposed to dissension.

Following the Ascension and Pentecost, Mary Magdalene's role will be to play a part in the conversion of the
gentiles.[318] As an "apostelesse," she is shown in the *Hunt-
ingfield Psalter* (Pierpont Morgan Library MS. M43), illuminated in the early thirteenth century, which illustrates her
speaking to a seated group (fol. 26ᵛ).[319] In the Digby play,
she is commissioned (by no less than Raphael, who is sent
to her from Christ in heaven) to proclaim the good news of
Christianity to the King of Marcylle in Provence. Other accounts tend to give her a more subordinate role in the conversion of the region that is now southern France,[320] but the
play uniquely sends her forth without companions on a ship
from the Holy Land to Marcylle to do this work.

Upon her arrival, Mary protests to the king that she is

not there for "decepcyon," but rather she has been sent by her heavenly Lord to reform man's "mysbele[f]" (ll. 1466, 1469). In an earlier scene, the fraudulent nature of the old religion of the country—a religion devoted to "Mahound," whose service is led by a fat priest and a scatologically-minded boy—is exposed; the worship of the time and place is revealed to be devil worship, with a function in it given to relics of Mahound that his devotees may venerate and kiss (ll. 1144-1248). As the priest explains, the miracles which this cult can effect are the reverse of good—e.g., to make one blind permanently (l. 1240). The sacrifice and office of the day are pure sacrilege involving Mass parody, a lesson in pure gibberish, and even singing that goes "all owt of rule" (ll. 1227-29). Not surprisingly, the god Mahound is not able to speak in the presence of Mary Magdalene (l. 1546) since he is the source of the fraud that pervades this false religion. When she prays, the idol quakes, and thereafter the pagan temple is itself miraculously destroyed through a spectacular theatrical effect: *"Here xall comme a clowd from heven, and sett the tempyl on afyer . . . "*; then the pagan priest and his clerk *"xall synke"* (l. 1561*sd*). God has shown his power. The king takes to his bed in despair, and it is then that the vision-like appearance of the light-bearing Mary, dressed in a white mantle and accompanied by an angelic visitor, gives hope to the king and queen—hope that is reinforced by the news that the queen is pregnant with an heir.

That some aspects of the scenes represented in the play should not be seen in the English visual arts ought not perhaps surprise us, since this legendary material is essentially the stuff of Provençal legend rather than English story. Nevertheless, the Provençal account was filtered through such early English collections as the life of the Magdalen in the *South English Legendary,*[321] which provides, for example, a sharply visualized segment narrating the confrontation between the Magdalen and pagan religion in Marseille when "Heo gan to speke aȝen hore lawe · so uair reson and god/ that non ne couthe hure ȝiue answere · ac as gidi echmon stod" (ll. 73-74). Here, as in the play, she begins the process of converting the king and queen as they attempt to sacrifice to the pagan gods, and the process is completed when, following her visionary appearance to them, she is able to guarantee their wish to have an heir. However, continental art did try to visualize some of the details of the conversion of the king and queen of Marseille as they appear in her legendary life. Thus an altarpiece, dated 1431, by Lukas Moser at Tiefenbronn shows the arrival by boat of the Magdalen and her companions at Marseille, their appearance at the gates of the city, and, above, the vision-like appearance of Mary to the king and queen in their bedroom, in this case located directly above the city gates.[322]

The subsequent journey of the king and the queen to Jerusalem follows the medieval pattern of pilgrimage, beginning with their separation from their community and their temporary loss of temporal power or authority. Their experience of liminality is based on their trust in the Christian Trinity who is the source of all life and who has been revealed to them through the mediation of Mary Magdalene. This trust, which involves too the active invocation of the saint, is able to transcend even the disaster of death that appears to overcome the queen on her voyage, though in fact she also is miraculously able to complete her pilgrimage, visiting the stations of the cross and the sepulchre of Christ in Jersalem and receiving baptism. The hardships of the pilgrimage are instructive, since even the loss of life is miraculously changed to life assured of an eternal dimension in demonstration of the central paradox of Christianity. Reversing the pretensions of pride demonstrated by the aristocratic characters at the beginning of the play, the royal couple illustrates how their loss of kingdom and even life is ultimate gain, guaranteeing additionally a kingdom now converted from false paganism to Christianity. Before their return to Marcylle, Mary Magdalene, who has been ruling as their regent, urges the folk: "Aȝens God, be nothyng vereabyll—/ Thynk how he mad all thyng of nowth!" (ll. 1925-26). God is, as the previously cited illumination in the *De Lisle*

92

Psalter demonstrates, the center of the wheel of life.[323] He who is penitent and weeps for his sin will be raised to eternal life by him who "for vs dyyd on the rode tre!" (ll. 1931-38). When the king and queen return to Marcylle with their child and heir, they praise the Magdalen:

> Heyll be thou, Mary! Ower Lord is wyth the!
> The helth of ower sowllys, and repast contemplatyff!
> Heyll, tabyrnakyll of the blyssyd Trenite!
> (ll. 1939-41)

For this royal couple, Mary Magdalene has been the bearer of God's saving power which overcomes all human imperfection and all the frailty of the flesh, including even death; her person has indeed been for them (and for all who venerate her) the "tabyrnakyll of the blyssyd Trenite" as well as "covnfortabyll sokore for man and wyff!" (ll. 1941-42).

In the final segment of the play, Mary Magdalene, after blessing the King and Queen of Marcylle, departs from the scaffold representing that city to go forth into the nearby wilderness of Provence to spend the last years of her life in contemplation.[324] The setting is now her humble hermitage in "this deserte" (l. 1989), a scene commonly represented in art in the fifteenth and sixteenth centuries.[325] An illumination in an early fifteenth-century Sarum Book of Hours, Bodleian MS. Laud Lat. 15, fol. 20^v, shows her actually alone out in the wilderness among the mountains; the nimbed figure of the saint, who wears a blue mantle over her kirtle, is praying with her hands joined in the late medieval gesture for prayer.[326] The mountains in this illumination look as though they could easily have been adapted to a stage setting, while similar mountains were, of course, familiar as standard elements of stagecraft in the fifteenth and early sixteenth centuries.[327] Brueghel's engraving *Magdalena Poenitens* reveals the Magdalen within her humble shelter: she is contemplating a passage in a book, which is perhaps a breviary or a book of hours, while beside her are a crucifix and a human skull, which are standard meditative aids.[328] In the play, she announces that her purpose shall be

> My sowle from synne to save;
> I wyll evyr abyte me wyth humelyte,
>   And put me in pacyens, my Lord for to love.
>   In charyte my werkys I woll grave,
> And in abstynens all dayys of my lyfe.
>
> (ll. 1990-94)

With these words she rededicates herself to humility which is the root of all goodness, to patience, and to charity. Furthermore, she represents for her followers and for the audience of the Digby play the way of contemplation as a rigorous exercise of piety that detaches her from this world and brings her into direct contact with the realm of transcendence. We may believe that one of the cultic purposes of the Digby play is likewise to achieve a closeness with that transcendent order. Indeed, the play dramatizes scenes which show a saint engaged in the mystical experience—an experience that would not be available to all, though some reflection of her mystical experience may be a spiritual help even to the feeblest of Christians in the audience attending the production of this play.

Mary is, of course, traditionally linked with devotion and contemplation because in *Luke* 10.39-42 she devotes herself to hearing the words of Christ while her sister serves their guest. Jesus approves of her devotional stance above the practical housewifery of Martha. Thus, for medieval theology, Martha became the emblem of the active life, while from at least the time of St. Augustine Mary became a symbol of the preferred contemplative life and of mystical experience.[329] The association of the Magdalen with light is in fact an extension of this aspect of her sainthood; the luminescence which she has received from the deity through her contemplation of him is reflected outward among her followers, beginning with the first members of her cult, the King and Queen of Marcylle and their subjects. Now at the end of her life she will devote herself wholly and purely to the service of Truth. Through self-knowledge and penitence she had turned from selfish devotion to pleasure to a new devotion to Christ, whose teaching had taught her humility and charity and all the other virtues. Thus she eventually reached that plane which St. Bernard called "the summit of humility; where, standing on Sion as on a watch-tower, [she] may survey the truth."[330] Now the intensity of her contemplation is such that she will turn all her senses away from earthly things; foregoing even all "wordly fodys," she will live only on "the fode that commyt from heven on hye" (ll. 2000-01).

The *Golden Legend* reports that Mary's hermitage, a cave prepared for her by angels, was in a place where there was "no comfort of rennyng water ne solace of tree ne of herbes." This barren place was, however, habitable by her "bycause our redemer . . . had ordeyned for her refection celestyall: and no bodely metes."[331]

> And euery daye at euery houre canonycall she was lyft vp in th'ayer of th'angellis/ and herde the gloryous songe of the heuenly companyes wyth her bodely eeres/ Of whiche she was fedde and fylled with ryght swete metes, and thene was brought again by th'angellys vnto her propre place/ in suche wyse as she hadde no nede of corporall norysshyng.[332]

The Digby play shows Jesus, enthroned in a heaven stage—i.e., on a stage well above the platea and the other scaffolds—bidding angels to descend to lift Mary up and to feed her with celestial manna (ll. 2006-07). The Second Angel promises her that she "xall be receyvyd into the clowddes,/ Gostly fode to reseyve to thi savacyon" (ll. 2025-26), and she is raised up into the clouds with the angels where she hears the music of heaven. In particular the angelic song is a variant of an antiphon for Lauds on the Feast of the Assumption,[333] suggesting further that the machinery utilized for raising the Magdalen might well also have been the same as that used for staging the Assumption upon other occasions. In lines 2033-34, Mary Magdalene praises God who has delivered her "from hovngure and wexacyon"; "O gloryus Lord, in the is no fravddys nor no defame!" Thrice daily

95

will she be raised up thus into the heavens in ecstasy. A continental woodcut by Dürer shows her lifted up above the earth, her body now covered only by her long, streaming hair, and surrounded by angels, while on the ground below her is the small figure of a hermit who shall "*spye Mari in hyr devocyon.*" The holy man who witnesses her ascension in the Digby play exclaims: "Grett art thou with God for thi perfythnesse!" (ll. 2044*sd*, 2048). *Queen Mary's Psalter* contains a similar scene, with the Magdalen lifted up by angels to hear heavenly music played on a fidel and another instrument which is perhaps a cittern. The saint in this illustration is wearing a gown and is standing or kneeling in what would appear to be a large napkin.[334]

The time has come for Mary to receive her last Communion in preparation for her soul's permanent ascent into heaven where she will receive her "ryth enirytawns": her heavenly "crown" (l. 2074). Christ in heaven now sends forth two angels, first to the hermit, who happens to be a priest, and then to the Magdalen. The Second Angel addresses Mary: "Mary, be glad, and in hart strong/ To reseyve the palme of grett wytory" (ll. 2093-94). The priest then comes to give her "the bred of lyf" which will bring her soul "to euyrlastyng lyth" (ll. 2102-04). She prays that the gates of heaven might open to her, and in imitation of her Lord who has preceded her into death, she cries:

> *In manus tuas, Domine!*
>
> .   .   .
>
> *Commendo spiritum meum! Redemisti me,*
> *Domine Devs veritatis!*
>
> (ll. 2115, 2117-18)

She speaks no more. Her soul is received into heaven where she is awarded her crown while the angel choir sings "a mery song" (l. 2122)—the stage direction reads "*Gavdent in celis*"—rejoicing at the successful completion of her earthly pilgrimage. In the miniature in *Queen Mary's Psalter* to which reference has been made above, her bodily ascension in con-

templation to partake of the heavenly harmony is a prefigur-
ing of her soul's ascent to heaven. In the Digby play, the holy
hermit who witnesses her death rejoices at what he has seen
and vows to take Mary's body to his bishop to be properly
buried "Wyth alle reverens and solemnyte" (ll. 2127-30).

The burial is not shown, though it is represented in another miniature in *Queen Mary's Psalter* that illustrates two
men placing her body into a tomb in a church; above the
hand of God is extended in blessing.[335] Instead, at the end
of the play the hermit and priest turns to the audience to
announce rather abruptly that the play is now ended:

> Sufferens of this processe, thus enddyt the sentens
> That we have playyd in yower syth.
> Allemythty God, most of magnyfycens,
> Mote bryng yow to hys blysse so brygth,
> In presens of that Kyng!
>
> (ll. 2131-35)

If there is in this play any didactic purpose, it is lifted up and
transformed through a higher design that stresses the function of devotion directed toward a saint whose principal actions involve her own conversion and the conversion of
pagans. As suggested above, Mary Magdalene actually is to
be identified as the Church itself,[336] and hence her character
may in the end be said to encompass the members of the
audience as the action of the play, peformed on the East
Anglian place-and-scaffold stage, may in turn have seemed
physically to encompass them. In any case, the play, like
Mirk's sermon on the Magdalen, encourages men and women
to identify themselves with this saint, whose help may be
invoked to assist them to order their lives in imitation of the
saint who is the model of penitence.[337] In certain medieval
hymns, the Magdalen, like the Blessed Virgin herself, had
been called "the star of the sea," *stella maris.* [338] The play
of *Mary Magdalene* in the Digby manuscript is another document which shows the saint pointing the way to brightest
bliss, which indeed is the devotional orientation of the medieval Church.

IX

The second saint play in Digby MS. 133 is the early sixteenth-century *Conversion of St. Paul,* which begins on fol. 38 and continues through fol. 50, including the section on fols. 45-47 that contains the added Belial scene from c.1550.[339] The dialect of the play is East Anglian or East Midland, suggesting that scribes and authors may have been from an area in the Bury St. Edmunds or Cambridge region.[340] John Coldewey's interesting speculation concerning a connection between the Digby plays and Chelmsford, Essex, has been mentioned above. The name of "Myles Blomefylde" across the top of the first page of the play has suggested to Coldewey that the play may have been one of those revived in this town in 1562 when a group of plays, unnamed in the records, was known to have been produced here.[341] In any case, Coldewey's argument is far more plausible for a play on the topic of the conversion of St. Paul than for production of the Digby *Mary Magdalene,* especially since St. Paul's story is more closely connected to the Bible than the other saint play in the Digby manuscript. However, certain restraints would still have applied, and any presentation of a saint play from a Catholic perspective (as opposed to a Protestant perspective) at this time would have been controversial. If the Digby *Conversion of St. Paul* was in fact included among the Chelmsford plays, the official attitude toward the cult of the saints might conceivably have helped to make the Chelmsford theatrical venture in 1562 such a financial disaster, assuming that such plays as the Digby *Conversion of St. Paul* were produced.

St. Paul the apostle, though in a sense more popular after the Reformation than before because of theological issues affecting Protestantism, nevertheless had been strongly represented in medieval church dedications and in the visual arts in England, particularly in association with St. Peter. At least twenty-nine churches are dedicated to him, while 275 are also dedicated to SS. Peter and Paul together.[342] The feast of the Conversion of St. Paul would seem to be the

correct occasion for the presentation of the Digby play; however, the date of this feast, 25 January, would hardly have
been propitious for an outdoor production, which the text of
the play seems unquestionably to demand. Hence it is much
more likely that the Commemoration of St. Paul on 30 June,
as established in the Sarum calendar, would have formed the
occasion for the original performances.[343]

The staging of the *Conversion of St. Paul* has been the
focus of considerable argument.[344] Raymond Pentzell has
argued for conventional processional staging at three locations[345] in a paper that would seem quite convincing except
for the fact of the reappearance of the priests Caypha (Caia-
phas) and Anna (Annas) in the final section of the play, suggesting rather that the play must spatially be able to double
back on itself—i.e., the audience may participate in the processional action of the play, while that procession (like many
religious processions such as the procession on the Feast of
St. Catherine at St. Paul's Cathedral in London reported by
Machyn[346]) does not really leave the area where the action
started. What we most likely have, then, is place-and-scaffold staging such as was commonly documented in East Anglia, though probably not in the *Castle of Perseverance* pattern
for which Mary del Villar argues.[347]

Whatever movement was involved (and surely this play
was not static in the way that del Villar suggests), the play
in fact combines processional movement with playing at stations and mansions or houses, with riding on horseback, and
with the appearance of God above on a raised stage. St.
Paul's sermon could well have been spoken either from a
cross in a marketplace or from a churchyard cross, which
was frequently used as a location for preaching.

Following the apparently optional appearance of the
Poeta (and possibly the dance indicated by a late hand in the
manuscript), the opening tableau of the play shows the saint
prior to his conversion (and hence named Saul instead of
Paul) coming before Caypha and Anna, who are described
in the stage directions as "*prestys of the tempyll*" entering
as aristocratic "prelatys" of the old order being upheld by

Saul's actions (ll. 35*sd,* 36). From them Saul receives letters, perhaps in the way depicted in two miniatures in *Queen Mary's Psalter,* fols. 240[v] and 302[v], though in the miniatures in this book he is kneeling in each case and accepting the letter (with its seal attached) from a single crowned figure (seated, as also would not have been likely in the play) while two or three knights in fourteenth-century armor stand behind him.[348] In the play, Saul is described as *"goodly besene in the best wyse, lyke an auenterous knyth"* (l. 14*sd*). His attendants, both subordinate knights and servants, appear with him. He is further a dreaded soldier and a "champyon" (l. 151) of the old ways against that which he perceives as a threat. Thus, as a knight prepared for conflict, we might expect him to be dressed in armor and ready to do battle. Saul in battle armor and with a sword is not unusual in iconography, as the famous miniature by Jean Fouquet showing the conversion scene in the *Hours of Etienne Chevalier* serves to illustrate.[349] The figure of Saul is apparently also signified by a man in armor in the cloisters of Norwich Cathedral, where a boss shows a person falling from his horse.[350] Aside from the armor, however, he is normally imagined to have been a small, bandy-legged man who is balding and with a long nose, as, for example, in the head shown in the fourteenth-century wall painting at Selling, Kent,[351] or the figure in painted glass of c.1515-20 in the south transept of York Minster.[352] John Capgrave, of King's (then Bishop's) Lynn in Norfolk, described the head of the saint, venerated as a relic at Rome, as having "a long face" and "balled with red her both berd and hed."[353]

In the Digby play, the trip to Damascus will not begin by foot, the means of locomotion shown in earliest extant illustrations which go back to the sixth century,[354] but instead Saul will travel by horse, usually anachronistically fitted with stirrups. Riding, which may have been introduced into the visualization of the story in the fourteenth century,[355] was, however, common enough in the late Middle Ages as the means of travel that Saul chooses for the journey on the road to Damascus. In the miniature by Fouquet and in painted glass in the Bowet Window in the choir of York Minster, he is riding a horse as he falls to the ground at the dramatic moment of his conversion.[356] In the play, a servant retrieves Saul's "palfray" from the groom, who provides him with the "best horse" in his stable (ll. 83, 121). On this horse Saul will set forth from this "stacyon" of Jerusalem, presumably with the audience following his movement to the next location.

The scene of St. Paul's conversion is fairly frequently illustrated in English art. Unfortunately, though this scene in the painted glass noted above—glass possibly painted by John Thornton of Coventry—in the choir of York Minster is very patched, James Torre in the seventeenth century provided a description of it: "Representation of St Paul's Conversion who is pictured falling backwards upon his white horse cast upon the ground as stricken by 2 great beams of Light . . . issuing out of a Cloud."[357] In the fourteenth-century *St. Mary's Psalter,* fols. 241 and 303, the conversion scene is shown twice, in each instance with the saint falling from his horse. In the first of these miniatures, five or six knights who are riding with him have difficulty controlling their horses as the light radiates down upon him from above where the head of Christ with a cross nimbus looks down.[358] In the other miniature, St. Paul, balding and bearded, tumbles from his mount. Two knights in contemporary armor riding on horses with saddles and stirrups are before him and three are behind, one of whom has his visor down and on his shield a demonic creature with large ears and sticking out its tongue. The saint, however, is dressed in a gown rather than armor,[359] and he is barefooted. In the Digby play, he surely would have removed any armor he might have worn after line 210 when apparently he goes into a booth, but then he will further change clothing into appropriate *"dyscyplys wede"* for his appearance at line 501. The play must have presented a fairly sensational effect when *"commyth a feruent* [i.e., lightning], *wyth gret tempest,"* whereupon the knight *"faulyth down of hys horse"* and *"Godhed spekyth in heuyn"* (l. 182sd).

101

Saul's blindness and lameness following his fall (literally a fall from pride into humility) requires that he seek help to go on to Damascus. Christ now must be in a position to appear to Ananias in Damascus, for this Christian must be appealed to and commissioned to look after the newly converted man who at this point shall be found "in humble vyse,/ As a meke lambe that a wolf before was namyd" (ll. 217-18). Presumably Christ has come down out of heaven to appear to Ananias, for the stage direction at l. 244 indicates that he should thereafter leave the playing area (*"Et exiat Deus"*). Ananias finds Saul in contemplation "in thys place and goodly mansyon" (l. 269). Paul was generally known as a contemplative, an identification insisted upon by the *Golden Legend* and appropriate for a saint who has been "rauysshed vnto the thyrde heuen"[360] and whose emblems are the book of the Gospel and the sword that is not only the sign of his martyrdom but also a hieroglyph of his evangelical efforts to communicate the mystical vision which he has experienced.[361] In his blindness, the scales had already fallen from the eyes of his spirit, and though he was physically blind he paradoxically could see better than previously. After he further receives his physical sight again, he asks Ananias for baptism "at the watery streme" (ll. 308-09).

While the text suggests that the baptism should take place at a stream or brook, the evidence of iconography would suggest that in fact some kind of baptismal font could nevertheless have been used.[362] Adult baptisms were often schematically illustrated in the arts, with persons receiving baptism actually standing nude in the font, as in the case of St. Paul himself in *Queen Mary's Psalter*, fol. 304v.[363] Of course, in this instance the presentation of such a tableau in early performances of the play is not at all likely. Instead, it would appear that Saul would kneel before the font as in the painted glass showing the baptism of St. Thomas Becket's mother in the painted glass at York, where the clergyman is pouring water over her head from a vessel.[364] However, even before his baptism and prior to the receipt of his sight again, the dove of the Holy Spirit has descended upon him—an effect similar to the descent of the dove in the Pentecost plays of the extant civic cycles. In the York play, for example, Peter comments on the vision of music and light as bright as the sun when the Holy Ghost is revealed to the apostles.[365] In the N-town *Pentecost,* a play most likely from the same region in England as the Digby *Conversion of St. Paul,*[366] the reaction of the apostles responding to the revelation of the Holy Spirit through the dove is theatrically quite simple, with the apostles at first genuflecting as the dove descends. Following a prayer they kiss the earth, and the Jews comment on them unfavorably. The playlet ends with Peter's speech of reproach to the Jews for their hostile words.[367] The effect at this point in the Digby play is simpler than in these Pentecost plays, though the emphasis is unquestionably on the illumination which is achieved through the revelation of the Holy Spirit. There is, however, no music, and the presence of light is only implied by the Digby text at line 294 as the dove descends upon Saul, who through this event and his baptism will even have his name changed. As noted, the technical effects need not be complicated. Undoubtedly similar to the working of the dove of the Holy Spirit at Lucerne in the latter part of the sixteenth century, the Digby production would have had a person assisting at the performance of the play whose job was to be the "operator" of the dove or Holy Spirit.[368] Saul then kneels for the "crystenyng," taking the posture normally adopted for adult baptism and being brought through this "sacrament" into the community of the early Church, whereupon the late stage direction added to the play indicates another *"Daunce"* (l. 345sd). A joyful conclusion to this scene is, of course, entirely appropriate.

The third scene is at a third station, described by the Poeta as "thys lytyll stacyon" (l. 363), presumably again at Jerusalem, where the soldiers report to the chief priests Caypha and Anna *"in the temple"* (l. 366sd). The priests are, to say the least, unhappy about the conversion of Saul "from our law" (l. 382). Here the mid-sixteenth-century addition of Belial and Mercury is inserted, the first entering *"wyth thunder and fyre"* (l. 412sd) in a sensational introduction and then being joined by the second *"wyth a fyeryng, commyng in hast, cryeng and roryng"* (l. 432*sd*). Their extreme discomfiture is, of course, an extension of the laments of the chief priests over the loss of their champion Saul, and further their invoking of the Seven Deadly Sins looks forward to St. Paul's sermon which follows in the play, perhaps, as noted above, at a market cross or preaching cross in a churchyard.

The iconography of Paul as a preacher is well established[369] and appears widely in the visual arts from the twelfth and thirteenth centuries, when the subject is shown in several extant English miniatures,[370] to the Reformation. The Bowet Window in the York Minster choir, probably painted by John Thornton, includes such a scene from the early fifteenth century.[371] The topic of St. Paul's sermon is likewise iconographically significant, since it draws on the idea of the Seven Deadly Sins as the fruits of the Tree of Evil (*Arbor Mala*), which not infrequently appears in iconographic representations in the visual arts (e.g., in the fragmentary wall paintings at Kentford, Suffolk).[372] The sermon is interrupted at the point at which St. Paul is proclaiming that "the Iey ys euer the messenger of foly" (l. 571), a traditional adage herein presented as evidence of his wisdom. His arrest by the servants of the priests thereafter leads to his imprisonment by Caypha and Anna within the city, from which he will eventually escape as a result of a warning by an angel. The escape, traditionally from the city of Damascus in a basket,[373] will not, however, be dramatized at the conclusion of the play. "Thus leve we Saule wythin the cyte,/ The gatys kep by commandment of Caypha and Anna," the Poeta curiously explains at the end, whereupon he adds the information that thereafter Paul will indeed escape by means of a basket and then join himself with the other disciples in Jerusalem. The playwright has surely missed a chance here to produce another spectacular scene comparable to the theatricality of the fall of Saul from his horse.

Unlike the Digby *Mary Magdalene,* no episodes from the legendary or apocryphal life of the saint will be appended to the narrative told in the play. It is not a bare biblical narrative, though its borrowings from other sources are less intrusive than we would expect. The result is a drama for which Arnold Williams thought some apology was needed in spite of its historical interest.[374] Indeed the *Conversion of St. Paul* is extremely valuable because of its historical significance, since, along with the Digby *Mary Magdalene* and the Cornish *St. Meriasek,* it represents a rich theatrical genre of which so little remains for all of England.

NOTES

[1]Harold C. Gardiner, *Mysteries' End* (New Haven, 1946; rpt. Archon Books, 1967), p. 54. For previous studies of the saint play, see George R. Coffman, "The Miracle Play in England," *Studies in Philology,* 16 (1919), 56-66; J. M. Manly, "The Miracle Play in Mediaeval England," *Essays by Diverse Hands,* n.s. 7 (1927), 133-53; Hardin Craig, *English Religious Drama* (Oxford: Clarendon Press, 1955), pp. 320-34; David L. Jeffrey, "English Saint Plays," *Medieval Drama,* ed. Neville Denny, Stratford-upon-Avon Studies, 16 (London: Edward Arnold, 1973), pp. 69-89. Problems of terminology are discussed by George R. Coffman, "The Miracle Play in England—Nomenclature," *PMLA,* 31 (1916), 448-65. The present study was supported in part by a fellowship and grant from the Faculty Research Fund of Western Michigan University, and additionally a sabbatical leave in 1983-84 made possible its completion.

[2]Gardiner, p. 54.

[3]Karl Young, *The Drama of the Medieval Church* (Oxford: Clarendon Press, 1933), II, 361-69.

[4]*Gesta Abbatum Monasterii Sancti Albani,* ed. Henry T. Riley, Rerum Britannicarum Medii Aevi Scriptores, 28 (London: Longmans, Green, 1867), I, 73. See also Catherine B. C. Thomas, "The Miracle Play at Dunstable," *Modern Language Notes,* 32 (1917), 337-44, and M. Dominica Legg, *Anglo-Norman Literature and Its Background* (Oxford: Clarendon Press, 1963), pp. 311-12.

[5]*York,* ed. Alexandra F. Johnston and Margaret Rogerson, Records of Early English Drama (Toronto: Univ. of Toronto Press, 1979), I, 289, 310-11, 318, 320, 326-27.

[6]Eileen White, " 'Bryngyng Forth of Saynt George': The St. George Celebrations in York," *Medieval English Theatre,* 3 (1981), 114-21.

[7]*York,* ed. Johnston and Rogerson, I, 68; *Testamenta Eboracensia,* Part II, ed. James Raine, Surtees Soc., 30 (Durham, 1855), p. 117.

[8]White, " 'Bryngyng Forth of Saynt George'," p. 118.

[9]Alan H. Nelson, *The Medieval English Stage* (Chicago: Univ. of Chicago Press, 1974), p. 52; on the Creed Play, also noted in Revetour's will, see especially Alexandra F. Johnston, "The Plays of the Religious Guilds of York: The Creed Play and the Pater Noster Play," *Speculum,* 50 (1975), 57-70.

[10]*Letters of the Kings of England,* ed. James Orchard Halliwell (London, 1848), I, 354; *York,* ed. Johnston and Rogerson, II, 649-50.

[11]See *York,* ed. Johnston and Rogerson, II, 649.

[12]A. C. Cawley, "The Sykes Manuscript of the York Scriveners' Play," *Leeds Studies in English,* n.s. 7-8 (1952), 45-80; for the text of the Scriveners' play, see *The York Plays,* ed. Richard Beadle (London: Edward Arnold, 1982), pp. 366-72.

[13]*York,* ed. Johnston and Rogerson, I, 88; *Testamenta Eboracensia,* Pt. II, p. 117n.

[14]Clifford Davidson and David E. O'Connor, *York Art,* Early Drama, Art, and Music,

CLIFFORD DAVIDSON

Reference Ser., 1 (Kalamazoo: Medieval Institute Publications, 1978), p. 152; *An Inventory of the Historical Monuments in the City of York, V: The Central Area* (Royal Commission on Historical Monuments, 1981), p. 17.

[15]Davidson and O'Connor, *York Art,* p. 152; James Torre, *Antiquities Ecclesiastical of the City of York,* York Minster Library MS., p. 471. See also Angelo Raine, *Mediaeval York* (London: John Murray, 1955), p. 106.

[16]Other examples at York include figures in painted glass in York Minster, where the saint's martyrdom is shown in a nave window, and in St. Martin, Coney Street, the latter lost in the bombing in World War II. The St. Martin's glass was dated c.1450, which would make it of approximately the same date as the play. See Davidson and O'Connor, p. 152. For a further example at Methley, Yorkshire, see James Fowler, "On the Painted Glass at Methley, Part II," *Yorkshire Archaeological Journal,* 2 (1873), 230.

[17]Sumner McKnight Crosby, *The Abbey of St.-Denis, 475-1122* (New Haven: Yale Univ. Press, 1942), I, 24-40; David Hugh Farmer, *The Oxford Dictionary of Saints* (Oxford: Clarendon Press, 1978), p. 106.

[18]E. G. Ryan, "St. Denis of Paris," *New Catholic Encyclopedia,* IV, 765-66.

[19]Jacobus de Voragine, *The Legend named in Latin "Legenda Aurea,"* trans. William Caxton (Westminster, 1493), fol. ccc^v; see also *The South English Legendary,* Pt. II, ed. Charlotte d'Evelyn and Anna J. Mill, EETS, o.s. 236 (1956), p. 439.

[20]E. W. Tristram, "The Cloister Bosses of Norwich Cathedral," [Norwich Cathedral] *Friends' Annual Report,* 7 (1936), 14; see also National Monuments Record archive (notes attached to Photo A66/703).

[21]Otto Pächt and J. J. G. Alexander, *Illuminated Manuscripts in the Bodleian Library, Oxford, 3: British, Irish, and Icelandic Schools* (Oxford: Clarendon Press, 1973), No. 540, Pl. LIII.

[22]Translation from *York,* ed. Johnston and Rogerson, II, 755; the original document lists "ij ludentibus de parochia Sancti Dionisij" who are paid 4d (ibid., I, 77).

[23]Philip Morant, *The History and Antiquities of the County of Essex* (London, 1768), II, 399.

[24]Ibid., II, 399.

[25]Ibid., II, 399. Morant's account is corroborated by a transcription from the Braintree churchwardens' accounts made by Samuel Drake (1680-1730); see W. A. Mepham, "Mediaeval Plays in the 16th Century at Heybridge and Braintree," *Essex Review,* 55 (1946), 14-15.

[26]Ibid., p. 15.

[27]Ibid., p. 15.

[28]Sidney Lee, "Nicholas Udall," *DNB,* XX, 6-9; Hartley S. Brook, *The Story of the Parish Church of St. Michael, Braintree* (Gloucester: British Publishing, n.d.), p. 23. E. K. Chambers erroneously gives Udall's tenure as vicar of Braintree as 1533-37 (*The Mediaeval Stage* [London: Oxford Univ. Press, 1903], II, 342).

[29]Farmer, *Oxford Dictionary of Saints,* p. 365; *South English Legendary,* Pt. I, ed. Charlotte d'Evelyn and Anna J. Mill, EETS, o.s. 235 (1956), p. 275.

[30]Farmer, *Oxford Dictionary of Saints,* p. 17. For further study of this apostle and saint, see especially Francis Dvornik, *The Idea of Apostolicity in Byzantium and the Legend of the Apostle Andrew,* Dumbarton Oaks Studies, 4 (Cambridge: Harvard Univ. Press, 1958), esp. pp. 138-299. The iconography, which appears most elaborately in the painted glass at Greystoke, Cumberland, is treated in Thomas Lees, "On the Stained Glass in the East Window of the Chancel of Greystoke Church," *Transactions of the Cumberland and Westmoreland Antiquarian and Archaeological Society,* 2 (1876), 375-89.

[31]Farmer, *Oxford Dictionary of Saints,* p. 144; Frances Arnold-Forster, *Studies in Church Dedications* (London: Skeffington, 1899), III, 361.

[32]*Legenda Aurea,* trans. Caxton, fol. cccxxiv.

106

[33]On the exclusion of persons with Irish surnames from guilds in Dublin, see John. J. Webb, *The Guilds of Dublin* (London: Ernest Benn, 1929), p. 70.

[34]Chambers, *Mediaeval Stage*, II, 365; on an English legend which connected these saints with Faversham, see Farmer, *Oxford Dictionary of Saints*, p. 93.

[35]Stanley J. Kahrl, ed., *Records of Plays and Players in Lincolnshire*, Malone Soc. Collections, VIII (1974), pp. 24-25.

[36]Young, *Drama of the Medieval Church*, I, 456-58; *Breviarium . . . ad usum insignis ecclesie Sarum* (Paris, 1531), fol. cxxviii.

[37]See Virginia Shull, "Clerical Drama in Lincoln Cathedral, 1318 to 1561," *PMLA*, 52 (1937), 949-50; see also Young, *Drama of the Medieval Church*, I, 449, 463ff, 466ff.

[38]*Records of Plays and Players in Lincolnshire*, p. 25.

[39]Ibid., p. 25.

[40]Shull, "Clerical Drama in Lincoln Cathedral," p. 951. The play of the Resurrection noted in the cathedral accounts for 1383-84 would not necessarily, however, have referred to a drama on the topic of the Resurrection itself, since the Emmaus and Doubting Thomas scenes were themselves considered to be "Resurrection" stories.

[41]*Records of Plays and Players in Lincolnshire*, p. 30; Bede, *A History of the English Church and People*, trans. Leo Sherley-Price (Harmondsworth: Penguin, 1955), p. 196.

[42]Farmer, *Oxford Dictionary of Saints*, pp. 237-38.

[43]Davidson and O'Connor, *York Art*, p. 162. See also the example in wall painting at Widford, Oxfordshire, noted by A. Caiger-Smith, *English Medieval Mural Paintings* (Oxford: Clarendon Press, 1963), p. 169, and the alabaster noted by M. D. Anderson, *Drama and Imagery in Medieval English Churches* (Cambridge: Cambridge Univ. Press, 1963), p. 201, at Lanteglos-by-Fowey, Cornwall, which shows an executioner with a beer mug beside him.

[44]Anderson, *Drama and Imagery*, pp. 200-01.

[45]T. Dineley, *An Account of the Progress of His Grace Henry the First Duke of Beaufort through Wales, 1684* (1864), p. 19.

[46]Thomas Wright, *The History and Antiquities of the Town of Ludlow* (1852), as quoted by Edwin W. Ganderton and Jean Lafond, *Ludlow Stained and Painted Glass* (Ludlow: Friends of the Church of St. Lawrence, 1961), pp. 12-13.

[47]Ganderton and Lafond, p. 13.

[48]Ibid., pp. 15-16; see also Anderson, *Drama and Imagery*, pp. 200-01.

[49]*Records of Plays and Players in Lincolnshire*, p. 31.

[50]Anderson, *Drama and Imagery*, pp. 61-62.

[51]J. Payne Collier, *The History of English Dramatic Poetry to the Time of Shakespeare* (1831; rpt. New York: AMS Press, 1970), I, 114-15; *Chester*, ed. Lawrence M. Clopper, Records of Early English Drama (Toronto: Univ. of Toronto Press, 1979), p. 484. On the legend of Robert of Sicily and extant texts in Middle English, see Laura A. Hibbard, *Mediaeval Romance in England*, revised ed. (New York: Burt Franklin, 1963), pp. 58-64.

[52]*Chester*, ed. Clopper, p. 26. The letter may suggest performance in Chester on the feast of St. Peter *ad vincula*, 1 August.

[53]*Records of Plays and Players in Lincolnshire*, p. 32.

[54]E. Clive Rouse and Audrey Baker, "Wall Paintings in Stoke Orchard Church, Gloucestershire, with Particular Reference to the Cycle of the Life of St. James the Great," *Archaeological Journal*, 123 (1966), 78-119.

[55]W. L. Hildburgh, "A Datable English Alabaster Altar-Piece at Santiago de Compostella," *Antiquaries Journal*, 6 (1926), 304-07, Pl. XLII.

[56]Francis Bond, *Dedications of English Churches* (Oxford: Humphrey Milford, 1914), p. 320.

[57]E. Clive Rouse, *St. James's Church, Stoke Orchard, Gloucestershire: Notes on the Church and Its Wall Paintings* (n.p., n.d.), p. 7. On medieval pilgrimage in relation to the cult of St.

James, see especially Jonathan Sumption, *Pilgrimage: An Image of Medieval Religion* (London: Faber and Faber, 1975).

[58]Denis Bethell, "The Making of a Twelfth-Century Relic Collection," in *Popular Belief and Practice,* ed. G. J. Cuming and Derek Baker (Cambridge: Cambridge Univ. Press, 1972), pp. 67, 69. Further information concerning this relic is contained in K. Leyser, "Frederick Barbarossa, Henry II, and the Hand of St James," *English Historical Review,* 90 (1975), 491-99, and in Brian Kemp, "The Miracles of the Hand of St. James," *Berkshire Archaeological Journal,* 65 (1970), 1-19.

[59]Sumption, *Pilgrimage,* p. 208; J. Toulmin Smith, *English Gilds,* EETS, e.s. 40 (1870), p. 180.

[60]H. F. Westlake, *The Parish Gilds of Mediaeval England* (London: SPCK, 1919), pp. 17, 169. At Ludlow, there was even a Guild of Palmers, though its principal devotion seems to have been to Edward the Confessor, whose legend forms the basis for the Palmers' Window in St. John Chapel in the parish church; see Ganderton and Lafond, pp. 46-53. The guild is discussed by W. C. Sparrow, "The Palmers' Gild of Ludlow," *Transactions of the Shropshire Archaeological Society,* 1 (1878), 333-94.

[61]See especially Victor Turner and Edith Turner, *Image and Pilgrimage in Christian Culture: Anthropological Perspectives* (New York: Columbia Univ. Press, 1978), pp. 1-39.

[62]See Peter Brown, *The Cult of the Saints* (Chicago: Univ. of Chicago Press, 1981), p. 57 and passim.

[63]*Records of Plays and Players in Lincolnshire,* p. 32. The next year, a Pater Noster play was instituted (ibid.). For examples of St. Clare in English art, see Davidson and O'Connor, *York Art,* p. 150, and R. L. P. Milburn, *Saints and Their Emblems in English Churches* (Oxford: Blackwell, 1957), p. 57. In his note "Was There a Play on the Martyrdom of Hugh of Lincoln" (*Modern Language Notes,* 69 [1954], 31-34), Roger Sherman Loomis reviews the hypothesis that there may have been a further Lincoln play on the life of this figure and concludes that its presence is not supported by the evidence; see also Leo Spitzer, "Istos ympnos ludendo composuit," *Modern Language Notes,* 69 (1954), 383-84.

[64]David L. Jeffrey, "Franciscan Spirituality and the Rise of Early English Drama," *Mosaic,* 8, No. 4 (1975), 17-46.

[65]Ibid., p. 33; Carleton Browne, "An Early Mention of a St. Nicholas Play in England," *Studies in Philology,* 28 (1931), 594-601. Browne, however, suggests that the book which contains this sermon may be Dominican rather than Franciscan (p. 594).

[66]Clifford Davidson, ed., *A Middle English Treatise on the Playing of Miracles* (Washington: Univ. Press of America, 1981), pp. 12-13. For previous editions of this poem, see ibid., p. 26, n. 47. An alternative theory is that the poet was referring to wall paintings; see Rossell Hope Robbins, ed., *Historical Poems of the XIVth and XVth Centuries* (New York: Columbia Univ. Press, 1959), p. 335.

[67]Lawrence G. Craddock, "Franciscan Influences on Early English Drama," *Franciscan Studies,* 10 (1950), 408-15. On the poem, see further Nicholas Davis, "The Playing of Miracles, c. 1350 to the Reformation," Ph.D. dissertation (Cambridge University, 1978), pp. 124-31, and Jeffrey, "Franciscan Spirituality and the Rise of Early English Drama," pp. 36-40.

[68]For a survey of the surviving art, see A. G. Little, ed., *Franciscan History and Legend in English Mediaeval Art* (Manchester: Manchester Univ. Press, 1937), passim.

[69]Ibid., Chapter I, Pl. VI; see also Francis Joseph Baigent, "On the Church of St. John, Winchester, and the Paintings Discovered on the North Wall," *Journal of the British Archaeological Association,* 9 (1853), 7, Pl. 3.

[70]The source of the belief in Franciscan involvement may be traced to William Dugdale, *The Antiquities of Warwickshire* (London, 1656), p. 116, who reports that the Coventry pageants were "acted with mighty state and reverence by the Friers. . . ." Cf. 2nd ed., ed. William Thomas, p. 149, for reference to the visit of King Henry VII to Coventry in 1492 "to see the Plays acted by the Grey Friers, and much commended them." These passages are quoted from the 2nd ed. by Ingram, ed., *Coventry,* pp. 77, 558.

[71]*Coventry,* ed. Ingram, p. 100.

[72]Farmer, *Oxford Dictionary of Saints,* p. 77.

[73]Craig, *English Religious Drama,* p. 332.

[74]*Coventry,* ed. Ingram, pp. 128, 536.

[75]Ibid., p. xx.

[76]Ibid., pp. 74, 551.

[77]Ibid., p. xx.

[78]See Charles Phythian-Adams, *Desolation of a City: Coventry and the Urban Crisis of the Late Middle Ages* (Cambridge: Cambridge Univ. Press, 1979), pp. 118-22.

[79]Ibid., p. 121.

[80]See Arnold-Forster, *Studies in Church Dedications,* I, 120.

[81]*Gesta Abbatum Monasterii Sancti Albani,* I, 73; Thomas, "The Miracle Play at Dunstable," pp. 337-44.

[82]Interest in St. Catherine was apparently spurred in England initially by the Normans; see Thomas, "The Miracle Play at Dunstable," pp. 337-41.

[83]Christopher Wordsworth, "Inventories of Plate, Vestments, &c., belonging to the Cathedral Church of the Blessed Mary at Lincoln," *Archaeologia,* 53 (1892), 14.

[84]*Coventry,* ed. Ingram, p. 488.

[85]Geoffrey Templeman, *The Records of the Guild of the Holy Trinity, St. Mary, St. John the Baptist, and St. Katherine of Coventry,* Dugdale Soc., 19 (London: Oxford Univ. Press, 1944), II, 176. The chapel was located in the Church of St. Michael in the south aisle. The guild kept a candle before the image of the saint on her feast day.

[86]Ibid., II, 176.

[87]Arnold-Forster, *Studies in Church Dedications,* I, 119-20; Ethel Carleton Williams, "Mural Paintings of St. Catherine in England," *Journal of the British Archaeological Journal,* 3rd ser., 7 (1942), 20.

[88]Davidson and O'Connor, *York Art,* p. 144; Williams, "Mural Paintings of St. Catherine," p. 22; E. W. Tristram, *English Medieval Wall Painting: The Thirteenth Century* (London: Oxford Univ. Press, 1950), II, 614-15, Pls. 39-40.

[89]C. J. W. Winter, "Discovery of a Mural Painting in the Church at Sporle," *Norfolk Archaeology,* 7 (1871), 303-08; E. W. Tristram, *English Wall Painting in the Fourteenth Century* (London: Routledge and Kegan Paul, 1955), pp. 249-50.

[90]Anderson, *Drama and Imagery,* pp. 198-99.

[91]Tristram, *English Medieval Wall Painting: The Thirteenth Century,* II, 249-50; see also the drawing by Winter, published with his article in *Norfolk Archaeology,* Pl. facing p. 305.

[92]Anderson, *Drama and Imagery,* p. 199. See also Francis Cheetham, *English Medieval Alabasters, with a Catalogue of the Collection in the Victoria and Albert Museum* (Oxford: Phaidon-Christie's, 1984), pp. 87-88.

[93]Joan C. Lancaster, *Guide to St. Mary's Hall,* 2nd ed. (Coventry, 1982), p. 63.

[94]Williams, "Mural Paintings of St. Catherine," pp. 29-32.

[95]See Pierre Turpin, "Ancient Wall-Paintings in the Charterhouse, Coventry," *Burlington Magazine,* 35 (1919), 249n.

[96]British Museum M&LA 1914, 5-21, 1; compare the scene depicted in the wall painting at Pickering, Yorkshire, where the idol is a horned image before which a fire burns and the Emperor kneels; see G. H. Lightfoot, "Mural Paintings in St. Peter's Church, Pickering," *Yorkshire Archaeological Journal,* 13 (1895), 361ff.

[97]*Illustrated Catalogue of the Exhibition of English Medieval Alabaster Work* (London: Society of Antiquaries, 1863), p. 67, Pl. XXII; Philip Nelson, "Ancient Alabasters at Lydiate," *Transactions of the Historic Society of Lancashire and Cheshire,* 67 (1916), fig. 3; cf. Cheetham, *English Medieval Alabasters,* pp. 87-88.

109

[98]For an example of a small demon as an imperial advisor in the St. Catherine story in painted glass at York, see Davidson and O'Connor, *York Art,* p. 144. The demon crown is quite usual for another tyrant, Herod, as Miriam Skey has shown; see "Herod's Demon-Crown," *Journal of the Warburg and Courtauld Institutes,* 40 (1977), 274-76.

[99]Nelson, "Ancient Alabasters at Lydiate," figs. 2-8.

[100]Philip Nelson, "Saint Catherine Panels in English Alabaster at Vienna," *Transactions of the Historic Society of Lancashire and Cheshire,* 74 (1923), 129, Pl. I.

[101]Ibid., p. 129, Pl. II.

[102]Ibid., p. 130, Pl. IV. See also Philip Nelson, "The Woodwork of English Alabaster Retables," *Transactions of the Historic Society of Lancashire and Cheshire,* 72 (1921), Pl. facing p. 52, for the triptych in St. Catherine's Church, Venice, and Cheetham, *English Medieval Alabasters,* pp. 90-91, for similar examples in the Victoria and Albert Museum.

[103]Nelson, *Medieval English Stage,* p. 171.

[104]*A Chronicle of London from 1089 to 1483,* ed. N. H. Nicolas (London, 1827), p. 80.

[105]*Historical Manuscripts Commission,* XIII, Pt. 4 (London, 1892), 288; Chambers, *Mediaeval Stage,* II, 369.

[106]*Chronicles of London,* ed. Charles Lethbridge Kingsford (Oxford: Clarendon Press, 1905), pp. 234-35. See also especially the discussions by Sidney Anglo, "The London Pageants for the Reception of Katharine of Aragon: November 1501," *Journal of the Courtauld and Warburg Institutes,* 26 (1963), 53ff, and Gordon Kipling, *The Triumph of Honour* (Leiden: Leiden Univ. Press, 1977), pp. 73ff. On boy vs. girl actors/actresses, see Meg Twycross, "'Transvestism' in the Mystery Plays," *Medieval English Theatre,* 5 (1983), 131.

[107]*Chronicles of London,* ed. Kingsford, pp. 235-36.

[108]Francis Grose and Thomas Astle, *The Antiquarian Repertory* (1807-09), II, 260, transcribing the account in a manuscript in the College of Arms (MS. I M. 13, fols. 27-67). Further accounts of entertainments for Catherine of Aragon are listed in C. E. McGee and John C. Meagher, "Preliminary Checklist of Tudor and Stuart Entertainments: 1485-1558," *Research Opportunities in Renaissance Drama,* 25 (1982), 44-48.

[109]William Herbert, *The History of the Twelve Great Livery Companies of London* (London, 1837), II, 532, 535.

[110]Westlake, *Parish Gilds,* pp. 183-84.

[111]Henry Machyn, *The Diary,* ed. John Gough Nichols, Camden Soc., 42 (London, 1848), p. 49; cf. ibid., p. 119.

[112]John Wasson, "The Morality Play: Ancestor of Elizabethan Drama?" in *Drama in the Middle Ages,* ed. Clifford Davidson, C. J. Gianakaris, and John H. Stroupe (New York: AMS Press, 1982), pp. 316-27.

[113]The official position with regard to St. Thomas Becket was established in Henry VIII's proclamation of 16 November 1538; see Paul C. Hughes and James F. Larkin, *Tudor Royal Proclamations* (New Haven: Yale Univ. Press, 1964), I, 275-76, and also Tancred Borenius, *St. Thomas Becket in Art* (1932; rpt. Port Washington, New York: Kennikat Press, 1970), pp. 109-10. Cf. Arthur P. Stanley, *Historical Memorials of Canterbury,* 11th ed. (London: John Murray, 1887), pp. 250-56.

[114]Wasson, "The Morality Play: Ancestor of Elizabethan Drama?" p. 325.

[115]On the suppression of the cult, see Borenius, *St. Thomas Becket in Art,* pp. 109-10, and John Phillips, *The Reformation of Images* (Berkeley and Los Angeles: Univ. of California Press, 1973), pp. 70-72. See also the chapter by Peter Happé, below.

[116]*Records of Plays and Players in Norfolk and Suffolk, 1330-1642,* ed. David Galloway and John Wasson, Malone Society *Collections,* XI (1980-81), p. 38.

[117]Anderson, *Drama and Imagery,* p. 197; see Westlake, *Parish Gilds,* pp. 14-15.

[118]Westlake, *Parish Guilds,* p. 15.

[119]Ibid., pp. 15, 197-98.

[120]Francis Blomefield, *The History of the City and County of Nor[folk]* (1765), II, 797.

[121]Anderson, *Drama and Imagery,* p. 197, is apparently engaging in mere speculation when she suggests that plays dramatizing the life of St. Thomas Becket were "regularly" acted and that these productions "possibly inspired several bosses in the Cathedral which illustrate his martyrdom, including the very rare subject of Henry II being scourged by the monks of Canterbury before the martyr's shrine."

[122]*Records of Plays and Players in Norfolk and Suffolk,* p. 190.

[123]See Farmer, *Oxford History of Saints,* p. 378, and *Records of Plays and Players in Norfolk and Suffolk,* p. 190n.

[124]*Records of Plays and Players in Norfolk and Suffolk,* p. 142.

[125]Ibid. Wasson's note locates the possible play at St. Thomas' Chapel in "St. Mary's churchyard" (ibid., p. 142n); cf. Ian Lancashire, *Dramatic Texts and Records of Britain: A Chronological Topography to 1558* (Toronto: Univ. of Toronto Press, 1984), p. 344.

[126]Giles Dawson, *Records of Plays and Players in Kent, 1450-1642,* Malone Society Collections, VII (1965), p. 92; *Records of Lydd,* trans. and transcribed by Arthur Hussey and M. M. Hardy, ed. Arthur Finn (Ashford, Kent, 1911), p. 160.

[127]Canterbury City Accounts FA 2, fol. 411^r, and FA 12, fol. 369^v. See also Dawson, *Records of Plays and Players in Kent,* pp. 191-200. For references to Kent records in manuscripts, I am indebted to James Gibson, who is preparing an edition of the dramatic records of this county for publication by Records of Early English Drama.

[128]Canterbury City Accounts FA 15, fol. 77^v; cf. Chambers, *Mediaeval Stage,* II, 345.

[129]*Records of Plays and Players in Kent,* p. 189; cf. J. Brigstocke Sheppard, "The Canterbury Marching Watch with Its Pageant of St Thomas," *Archaeologia Cantiana,* 12 (1878), 27-46.

[130]*Records of Plays and Players in Kent,* pp. 191-98.

[131]"Midsummer Shows," ed. Jean Robertson and D. J. Gordon, in Malone Society Collections, III (1954), p. 3.

[132]Canterbury City Accounts FA 2, fol. 411^r, etc. Stage blood in Shakespeare's time was surely handled no differently; see Leo Kirschbaum, "Shakespeare's Stage Blood and Its Critical Significance," *PMLA,* 64 (1949), 517-25.

[133]Borenius, *St. Thomas Becket in Art,* p. 82, Pl. XIII.

[134]Ibid., Pl. XXX.

[135]British Museum M&LA90, 8-9, 1.

[136]John Gough Nichols and Thomas Fisher, *Ancient Allegorical, Historical, and Legendary Paintings in Fresco, discovered in the Summer of 1804, on the Walls of the Chapel of the Trinity, belonging to the Gilde of the Holy Cross, at Stratford-upon-Avon in Warwickshire* (London, 1838), Pl. XIV.

[137]Tristram, *English Wall Painting in the Fourteenth Century,* p. 18.

[138]Borenius, *St. Thomas Becket in Art,* p. 100, Pl. XLIV.

[139]Ibid., p. 73.

[140]Tristram, "The Cloister Bosses of Norwich Cathedral," p. 18.

[141]Madeline Harrison Caviness, *The Windows of Christ Church Cathedral, Canterbury,* Corpus vitrearum medii aevi: Great Britain, 2 (London: Oxford Univ. Press, 1981), p. 268, figs. 494, 494a. For further examples of the martyrdom in the visual arts, see Borenius, *St. Thomas Becket in Art,* pp. 70-104.

[142]*Legenda aurea,* trans. Caxton, fol. lxvi^v.

[143]"Midsummer Shows," ed. Robertson and Gordon, pp. 3-4n.

[144]*Legenda aurea,* trans. Caxton, fol. lxiii. See also the account in *The South English Legendary,* II, 610-15.

[145]George Warner, *Queen Mary's Psalter* (London: British Museum, 1912), Pl. 282; Bor-

CLIFFORD DAVIDSON

enius, *St. Thomas Becket in Art*, p. 40, Pl. X, fig. 1; Tancred Borenius, "Some Further Aspects of the Iconography of St. Thomas Becket," *Archaeologia*, 83 (1933), 178.

[146]Warner, *Queen Mary's Psalter*, Pl. 283; Davidson and O'Connor, *York Art*, p. 176.

[147]Peter Gibson, "The Stained and Painted Glass of York," in *The Noble City of York*, ed. Alberic Stacpoole et al. (York: Cerialis Press, 1972), pp. 198-99, Pl. 18A; Eric Milner-White, [York Minster] *Friends Annual Report*, 35 (1963), 14-16.

[148]Milner-White, *Friends Annual Report*, pp. 14-16.

[149]"Midsummer Shows," ed. Robertson and Gordon, pp. 3-4; William Tydeman, *The Theatre in the Middle Ages* (Cambridge: Cambridge Univ. Press, 1978), p. 139, fig. 10.

[150]*Paston Letters and Papers of the Fifteenth Century*, ed. Norman Davis (Oxford: Clarendon Press, 1971), I, 461.

[151]*York*, ed. Johnston and Rogerson, I, 318; White, " 'Bryngyng Forth of Saynt George'," pp. 116-19.

[152]*York*, ed. Johnston and Rogerson, I, 319; White, " 'Bryngyng Forth of Saynt George'," pp. 119-20, for further information about Stamper.

[153]*York*, ed. Johnston and Rogerson, I, 318.

[154]Davidson and O'Connor, *York Art*, pp. 156-58.

[155]Ibid., fig. 38.

[156]Ibid., pp. 156-57; J. B. Morrell, *Woodwork in York* (York, 1949), fig. 71.

[157]Davidson and O'Connor, *York Art*, p. 158; Pächt and Alexander, *Illuminated Manuscripts in the Bodleian Library*, III, Pl. LXXVII.

[158]Robert Johnson, *The Most Famous History of the seuen Champions of Christendome* (London, 1608), p. 2: "for the famous Cittie of *Couentrie* was the place wherein the first Christian Champion of England was borne, and the first that euer sought forraine aduentures, whose name to this day all Europe highly hath in regard, and for his bold and magnanimious deeds at armes gaue him this title, *The valiant Knight Saint George of England*, whose golden Garter is not onely worne by Nobles, but by kings: and in memorie of his victories, all *England* fights euermore vnder his banner."

[159]*Coventry*, ed. Ingram, p. 488.

[160]Charles Phythian-Adams, "Ceremony and the Citizen," in *Crisis and Order in English Towns, 1500-1700*, ed. Peter Clark and Paul Slack (Toronto: Univ. of Toronto Press, 1972), pp. 76-77.

[161]*Coventry*, ed. Ingram, pp. 54-55, 90.

[162]Ibid., p. 54. Reference may be made to the wall painting at the Guild Chapel at Stratford-upon-Avon, where the crowned princess was shown with a lamb and her parents were shown in their castle; see Fisher's drawing, Pl. XVII. An interlude and pageant of St. George and the Castle at Westminster were reported on Twelfth Night in 1494; see *The Great Chronicle of London*, ed. A. H. Thomas and I. D. Thornley (London, 1838), pp. 251-52.

[163]*Coventry*, ed. Ingram, p. 55.

[164]Ibid., p. 90.

[165]See J. Lewis André, "Saint George the Martyr in Legend, Ceremonial, Art, etc.," *Archaeological Journal*, 57 (1900), 206-07; Ethel Carleton Williams, "Mural Paintings of St. George," *Journal of the British Archaeological Association*, 3rd ser., 12 (1949), 20.

[166]*The Chronicles of Froissart*, trans. Lord Berners, ed. G. C. Macaulay (London: Macmillan, 1899), p. 82.

[167]The woodcarvings in the choir which treat the story of St. George have been discussed and identified by William St. John Hope, *Windsor Castle: An Architectural History* (London: Country Life, 1903), II, 429-73, and M. R. James, *The Woodwork of St. George's Chapel, Windsor* (Windsor, 1933), passim.

[168]*The Oxford Dictionary of the Christian Church*, ed. F. L. Cross, 2nd ed. (London: Oxford Univ. Press, 1974), p. 557.

112

[169]Bernard Andrew, *Historia Regis Henrici Septimi,* ed. James Gairdner, Rerum Britannicarum Medii Aevi Scriptores, 10 (London, 1858), p. 31; Robert Fabyan, *Chronicle,* p. 688; André, "Saint George the Martyr," p. 221.

[170]See, for example, Mervyn James, "Ritual, Drama and the Social Body in the Late Medieval English Town," *Past and Present,* No. 98 (1983), pp. 3-29. It is a shame that this otherwise valuable article fails to make use of recent scholarship such as the REED volumes and certain volumes in the Malone Society's *Collections* series.

[171]*Records of Plays and Players in Norfolk and Suffolk,* pp. 170-83.

[172]Ibid., pp. 175, 178-79.

[173]Ibid., p. 181; cf. ibid., p. 83, for citation of Nathaniel Bacon, whose *Annalls of Ipswiche* (1654) imply a terminal date of 1542 for the pageants.

[174]John Wasson, "Corpus Christi Plays and Pageants at Ipswich," *Research Opportunities in Renaissance Drama,* 19 (1976), 103.

[175]On the evidence for other saint pageants and perhaps plays on another festival in Norwich, see Norman Davis, ed., *Non-Cycle Plays and Fragments,* EETS, s.s. 1 (1970), p. xxvii. See also Nelson, *Medieval English Stage,* pp. 121-22.

[176]Three complete examples and an earlier head of Snap the dragon are currently on display in the Castle Museum, Norwich. See *The Norwich Snapdragon,* Norfolk Museums Service Information Sheet (Norwich, 1984); Robert Withington, *English Pageantry* (1918; rpt. New York: Benjamin Blom, 1963), I, 28 and illustration facing p. 29; W. C. Ewing, *Notices and Illustrations of the Costume, Processions, Pageantry, & c. formerly displayed by the Corporation of Norwich* (Norwich: Charles Muskatt, 1850), especially the plate facing p. 35 which shows a late seventeenth-century Snap. I am grateful to Rosemary Heaword for calling my attention to this illustration; see also her article "Snap the Dragon," *Albion,* No. 2 (1979), pp. 12-13.

[177]Westlake, *Parish Gilds,* p. 203; Toulmin Smith, *English Gilds* p. 445. A wall painting of St. George found in the parish church of St. Gregory perhaps also had guild associations; see Ernest A. Kent, "The Mural Painting of St. George in St. Gregory's Church, Norwich," *Norfolk Archaeology,* 25 (1933), 167-69.

[178]Smith, *English Gilds,* p. 445.

[179]*Records of the Gild of St. George in Norwich, 1389-1547,* ed. Mary Grace, Norfolk Record Soc., 9 (1937), p. 30. Cf. Chambers, *Mediaeval Stage,* I, 223; it is typical of Chambers that he totally ignores the important matter of the relic and notices only the angel, secondary in every way to the arm of the saint which was indeed of the greatest cultic significance.

[180]*Records of the Gild of St. George,* ed. Grace, pp. 31-32.

[181]*Norwich 1540-1642,* ed. David Galloway, Records of Early English Drama (Toronto: Univ. of Toronto Press, 1984), pp. 27-29.

[182]Ibid., p. 47; cf. *Records of the Gild of St. George,* ed. Grace, p. 140, for reference to making costumes for both St. George and St. Margaret in 1537.

[183]*Chester,* ed. Clopper, p. 8.

[184]*Records of Plays and Players in Kent,* p. 93.

[185]Ibid., pp. 199-200.

[186]Ibid., pp. 199, 133; see also W. A. Scott-Robertson, "The Passion Play and Interludes at New Romney," *Archaeologia Cantiana,* 13 (1880), 218-19.

[187]John Wasson, "The *St. George* and *Robin Hood Plays* in Devon," *Medieval English Theatre,* 2 (1980), 66-67.

[188]Chambers, *Mediaeval Stage,* II, 365-66; Nelson, *Medieval English Stage,* p. 186.

[189]Ibid., II, 365; cf. Withington, *English Pageantry,* I, 31-32.

[190]Chambers, *Mediaeval Stage,* II, 365-66; Withington, *English Pageantry,* I, 31-32; see also the seventeenth-century copy of the Chain Book in British Library MS. 4791, fol. 157.

[191]J. Charles Cox, *Churchwardens' Accounts* (London: Methuen, 1913), p. 270; see also

CLIFFORD DAVIDSON

B. Hale Wortham, "Churchwardens' Accounts of Bassingbourne," *The Antiquary,* 7 (1883), 25.

Ibid., p. 25.

[193]Ibid., p. 25.

[194]E. W. Tristram, *English Medieval Wall Painting: The Twelfth Century* (London: Oxford Univ. Press, 1944), p. 27, Pls. 31, 33; Williams, "Mural Paintings of St. George," pp. 22-23.

[195]James, *The Woodwork of St. George's Chapel, Windsor,* pp. 18-20, 31.

[196]Gordon McN. Rushforth, "The Windows of the Church of St. Neot, Cornwall," *Exeter Diocesan Architectural and Archaeological Society,* 15 (1937), 173-77, Pl. XLIV.

[197]Ibid., p. 174.

[198]Ibid., p. 174.

[199]Ibid., p. 177.

[200]Ibid., p. 176-77.

[201]Edward S. Prior and Arthur Gardner, *An Account of Medieval Figure-Sculpture in England* (Cambridge: Cambridge Univ. Press, 1912), fig. 537.

[202]Philip Nelson, "English Medieval Alabaster Carvings in Iceland and Denmark," *Archaeological Journal,* 77 (1920), Pl. VI.

[203]Ibid., Pl. VI.

[204]Arnold Taylor, "Royal Arms and Oblations in the Later 13th Century: An Analysis of the Alms Roll of 12 Edward I (1283-4)," in *Tribute to an Antiquary: Essays Presented to Marc Fitch by Some of His Friends,* ed. Frederick Emmison and Roy Stephens (London: Leopard's Head Press, 1976), p. 123; R. M. Wilson, *The Lost Literature of Medieval England* (1952; rpt. London: Methuen, 1970), pp. 231-32.

[205]R. E. Alton, "The Academic Drama in Oxford: Extracts from the Records of Four Colleges," Malone Society *Collections,* V (Oxford, 1960), p. 46.

[206]Chambers, *Mediaeval Stage,* II, 381; Andrew, *Historia Regis Henrici Septimi,* p. 121.

[207]W. D. Macray, *Historical Manuscripts Commission,* XV, Pt. 10 (London, 1899), 32; cf. H. Owen and J. B. Blakeway, *A History of Shrewsbury* (London, 1825), I, 328. See also Nelson, *Medieval English Stage,* pp. 186-87.

[208]*Churchwardens' Accounts at Betrysden, 1515-1573,* ed. Francis R. Mercer, Kent Record Soc., 5 (Ashford, Kent, 1928), pp. 3-5.

[209]*Records of Plays and Players in Lincolnshire,* p. 12; W. G. B[enham], " 'Seynt Martyns Pley' at Colchester," *Essex Review,* 48 (1939), 83.

[210]"Midsummer Shows," ed. Robertson and Gordon, pp. xx, 13-15, 18.

[211]Ibid., pp. xx, 13-15, 18.

[212]Machyn, *Diary,* pp. 47-48. In this case, the pageant was associated with a Lord Mayor's procession.

[213]See also, for example, Anna J. Mill, *Mediaeval Plays in Scotland* (1924; rpt. New York: Benjamin Blom, 1969), pp. 69, 271-72. Mill, pp. 276-81, further mentions a play of St. Tobert at Perth, but this saint is unidentified, though some have speculated that the reference is intended to refer to St. Cuthbert. There is also the very late dramatization of the legend of SS. Crispin and Crispinianus by the Shoemakers' Guild at Wells in 1613, and this drama (or quasi-dramatic pageant) presented by youths and girls may represent a sanitized version of a medieval play that had survived. See James Stokes, "The Wells Cordwainers Show: New Evidence Concerning Guild Entertainments in Somerset," *Comparative Drama,* forthcoming.

Lists of saints whose lives were given dramatizations in England, and of locations at which such plays were performed, are noted in footnotes 1 and 2 in John Wasson's chapter, below.

[214]"Midsummer Shows," ed. Robertson and Gordon, p. 14. On the St. Ursula legend and a connection with England through the alleged nationality of the saint and "Pope Cyriacus," see especially Osbern Bokenham, *Legendys of Hooly Wummen,* ed. Mary S. Serjeant-

114

son, EETS, o.s. 206 (1938), pp. 86-98, and M. Tout, "The Legend of St. Ursula and the Eleven Thousand Virgins," in *Historical Essays by Members of the Owens College, Manchester,* ed. T. F. Tout and James Tait (London: Longmans, Green, 1902), pp. 17-56.

[215]"Midsummer Shows," ed. Robertson and Gordon, pp. 33-34.

[216]*Non-Cycle Plays and Fragments,* pp. 100-13. For the play of St. Mary at New Romney, see *Records of Plays and Players in Kent,* p. 130.

[217]Constance B. Hieatt, "A Case for *Duk Moraud* as a Play of the Miracles of the Virgin," *Mediaeval Studies,* 32 (1970), 345-51. But see also Richard L. Homan, "Two Exempla: Analogues to the *Play of the Sacrament* and *Dux Moraud,*" *Comparative Drama,* 18 (1984), 241-51.

[218]Stephen K. Wright, "The Durham Play of Mary and the Poor Knight: Sources and Analogues of a Lost English Miracle Play," *Comparative Drama,* 17 (1983), 254-66.

[219]Ibid.

[220]*Coventry,* ed. Ingram, p. 488. See the jeer about the relics of "the Virgin Maries milke" in Barnabe Googe, *The Popish Kingdome* (London, 1570), fol. 37, and Erasmus' section on the milk of the Virgin at Walsingham in his "Pilgrimage for Religion's Sake" (*Colloquies,* trans. Craig R. Thompson [Chicago: Univ. of Chicago Press, 1965], pp. 295-96).

[221]Davidson and O'Connor, *York Art,* p. 184; see also Bethell, "The Making of a Twelfth-Century Relic Collection," p. 69. A girdle of the Blessed Virgin at Westminster Abbey was worn during difficult child-bearing by members of the royal family; see E. H. Pearce, *The Monks of Westminster* (Cambridge: Cambridge Univ. Press, 1916), pp. 35, 49, 72, 79.

[222]For treatment of the early life of the Virgin, see the N-town cycle, edited by K. S. Block under the title *Ludus Coventriae, or The Plaie called Corpus Christi,* EETS, e.s. 120 (1922), pp. 63-97. Proof of the controversial nature of the conclusion of the Virgin's life is the actual removal of this section from the Towneley manuscript; see Martin Stevens, "The Missing Parts of the Towneley Cycle," *Speculum,* 45 (1970), 254-65.

[223]Another play illustrating a miracle of the Virgin appears to have been the "*ludo de Mankynd, et aliis ludis*" noted in 1499 at East Retford, Nottinghamshire, for which an image of the Blessed Virgin Mary is cited, apparently as a stage property. See Siegfried Wenzel, "An Early Reference to a Corpus Christi Play," *Modern Philology,* 74 (1977), 393-94. An interlude in the Cornish *St. Meriasek* (ll. 3156-3802) dramatizes the Virgin's rescue of a woman's son from a tyrant following prayers spoken before her image, which depicted Mary holding her own Son; see *The Life of Saint Meriasek, Bishop and Confessor,* ed. and trans. Whitley Stokes (London: Trübner, 1872). For examples of extant iconography of the Virgin in the visual arts in England, see M. D. Anderson, *The Imagery of British Churches* (London: John Murray, 1955), pp. 146-47.

[224]The plays in the Digby Manuscript are reproduced in facsimile in *The Digby Plays,* introd. Donald C. Baker and J. L. Murphy, Leeds Texts and Monographs (Leeds: Univ. of Leeds School of English, 1976); they have been edited by Donald C. Baker, John L. Murphy, and Louis B. Hall, *The Late Medieval Religious Plays of Bodleian MSS Digby 133 and e museo 160,* EETS, 283 (1982).

[225]See, for example, B. Kurth, "Some Unknown English Embroideries of the Fifteenth Century," *Antiquaries Journal,* 23 (1943), 33.

[226]John Velz, "Sovereignty in the Digby Mary Magdalene," *Comparative Drama,* 2 (1968), 32-43; Theresa Coletti, "The Design of the Digby Play of *Mary Magdalene,*" *Studies in Philology,* 76 (1979), 313-33; Sister Nicholas Maltman, O.P., "Light In and On the Digby *Mary Magdalene,*" in *Saints, Scholars, and Heroes: Studies in Medieval Culture in Honour of Charles W. Jones,* ed. Margot H. King and Wesley M. Stevens (Collegeville, Minnesota: Hill Monastic Manuscript Library, 1979), I, 257-80.

[227]See Meyer Schapiro, "The Religious Meaning of the Ruthwell Cross," in *Late Antique, Early Christian and Mediaeval Art* (New York: George Braziller, 1979), pp. 163-64. Schapiro usefully notes that those elements derived from the story of St. Mary the Egyptian had already been "grafted on to the Magdalen's" legend in Anglo-Saxon England, perhaps due

to the encouragement of women ascetics who appeared so prominently in the country at that time (p. 164). See also J. E. Cross, "Mary Magdalen in the *Old English Martyrology*: The Earliest Extant 'Narrat Josephus' Variant of Her Legend," *Speculum*, 53 (1978), 16-20.

[228] Arnold-Forster, *Studies in Church Dedications*, I, 91; III, 19, 418-20.

[229] William Dugdale, *Monasticon Anglicanum*, revised ed., ed. John Caley, Henry Ellis, and Bulkeley Bandinel (London, 1817-30), II, 531; Victor Saxer, *Le Culte de Marie Madeleine en occident* (Paris: Librairie Clavreuil, 1959), I, 54; John Adair, *The Pilgrim's Way: Shrines and Saints in Britain and Ireland* (London: Thames and Hudson, 1978), p. 75; Herbert F. Westlake, *Westminster Abbey* (London: Philip Allan, 1923), II, 499.

[230] Sumption, *Pilgrimage*, p. 35.

[231] Patrick J. Geary, *Furta Sacra: Thefts of Relics in the Central Middle Ages* (Princeton: Princeton Univ. Press, 1978), pp. 90-95; Saxer, *Le Culte de Marie Madeleine*, I, 61ff.

[232] Bokenham, *Legendys of Hooly Wummen*, pp. 171-72; cf. Geary, *Furta Sacra*, p. 91.

[233] Gregory the Great, *Moralia in Job*, VI.28, as cited by Helen Meredith Garth, *Saint Mary Magdalene in Mediaeval Literature*, Johns Hopkins Univ. Studies in Historical and Political Science, ser. 67, No. 3 (1950), p. 19; Marjorie M. Malvern, *Venus in Sackcloth: The Magdalene's Origins and Metamorphoses* (Carbondale and Edwardsville: Southern Illinois Univ. Press, 1975), passim; Sister Mary John of Carmel Chauvin, "The Role of Mary Magdalene in Medieval Drama," Ph.D. dissertation (Catholic Univ. of America, 1951), pp. 2-4.

[234] *Breviarium . . . ad vsum insignis ecclesie Sarum*, fol. lxxxviii; *Legenda aurea*, trans. Caxton, fol. clxxxiv; Bokenham, *Legendys of Hooly Wummen*, pp. 144-72; *The South English Legendary*, I, 302-15.

[235] See Anselm Hufstader, "Lefèvre d'Étaples and the Magdalen," *Studies in the Renaissance*, 16 (1969), 31-35.

[236] *Confutation of Lefèvre's Second Disquisition*, as quoted by Edward Surtz, *The Works and Days of John Fisher* (Cambridge: Harvard Univ. Press, 1967), p. 287.

[237] *The Single Magdalene*, as cited by Surtz, *The Works and Days of John Fisher*, p. 277.

[238] *The Late Medieval Religious Plays*, p. xxx.

[239] Ibid., pp. xxxi-xxxii.

[240] Ibid., pp. 216-17.

[241] Jacob Bennett, "The *Mary Magdalene* of Bishop's [now King's] Lynn," *Studies in Philology*, 75 (1978), 1-9.

[242] Westlake, *Parish Gilds of Mediaeval England*, p. 217.

[243] *The Records of the City of Norwich*, ed. William Hudson and John C. Tingey (Norwich and London: Jarrold and Sons, 1906-10), II, cxxxv.

[244] Ibid., II, 120-21, 123.

[245] Ibid., II, 120-21.

[246] John Coldewey, "The Digby Plays and the Chelmsford Records," *Research Opportunities in Renaissance Drama*, 18 (1975), 103-21.

[247] *Visitation Articles and Injunctions of the Period of the Reformation*, ed. Walter H. Frere, Alcuin Club Collections, 16 (London: Longmans, Green, 1910), III, 16.

[248] Richard Beadle, "The Medieval Drama of East Anglia: Studies in Dialect, Documentary Records and Stagecraft," Ph.D. dissertation (Univ. of York, 1977), p. 234. Early consideration of the staging was undertaken by Victor E. Albright, *The Shaksperian Stage* (New York: Columbia Univ. Press, 1926), pp. 15-17, Pl. 3A. See also Glynne Wickham, "The Staging of Saint Plays in England," in *The Medieval Drama*, ed. Sandro Sticca (Albany: State Univ. of New York Press, 1972), pp. 111-15.

[249] *The Staging of Religious Drama in Europe in the Later Middle Ages: Texts and Documents in English Translation*, Early Drama, Art, and Music, Monograph Ser., 4 (Kalamazoo: Medieval Institute Publications, 1983), pp. 283-85 and fold-out diagram; A. M. Nagler, *The Medieval Religious Stage* (New Haven: Yale Univ. Press, 1976), pp. 30-31.

[250]Albright, *The Shaksperian Stage,* Pl. 3A; Bevington, *Medieval Drama,* p. 688.

[251]Beadle, "The Medieval Drama of East Anglia," pp. 236-37.

[252]E. K. Chambers, *English Literature at the Close of the Middle Ages* (London: Oxford Univ. Press, 1945), p. 64; cf. Chambers, *The Mediaeval Stage,* II, 154-55; Charles Mills Gayley, *Plays of Our Forefathers* (New York: Duffield, 1907), p. 208.

[253]Gregory the Great, *XL Homilarium in Evangelia,* II, 33; *PL* LXXVI.1238ff, as cited by Morton W. Bloomfield, *The Seven Deadly Sins* (East Lansing: Michigan State College Press, 1952), p. 73; see also Joseph Szövérffy, " 'Peccatrix quondam femina': A Survey of the Mary Magdalen Hymns," *Traditio,* 19 (1963), 134.

[254]*Jacob's Well,* ed. Arthur Brandeis, EETS, o.s. 115 (London, 1900), p. 185. See also *The South English Legendary,* I, 304; this and other parallels with this work have led Darryll Grantley to suggest it as a source for the play (see his "The Source of the Digby *Mary Magdalen,*" *Notes and Queries,* 31 [1984], 457-59). For a discussion of the identification of the seven devils with the Seven Deadly Sins in continental drama, see Chauvin, "The Role of Mary Magdalene," pp. 16-17.

[255]Gertrud Schiller, *Christian Iconography,* trans. Janet Seligman (Greenwich, Conn.: New York Graphic Soc., 1972), II, fig. 449.

[256]See Samuel Chew, *The Pilgrimage of Life* (New Haven: Yale Univ. Press, 1962), pp. 70-71; Siegfried Wenzel, "The Three Enemies of Man," *Mediaeval Studies,* 29 (1967), 47-66.

[257]See *Robert de Lisle Psalter,* British Library MS. Arundel 83, fol. 126^v; Adolf Katzen-ellenbogen, *Allegories of the Virtues and Vices in Mediaeval Art* (1939; rpt. New York: Norton, 1964), Pls. XLIV-XLV.

[258]Leon Eugene Lewis, "The Play of *Mary Magdalene,*" Ph.D. dissertation (Univ. of Wisconsin, 1963), p. 123, suggests a connection here with the Seven Deadly Sins.

[259]Roberto Salvini, *All the Paintings of Giotto,* trans. Paul Colacicchi (New York: Hawthorn, 1963), Pl. 169.

[260]See Anderson, *The Imagery of British Churches,* pp. 166-67.

[261]H. Arthur Klein, *Graphic Worlds of Peter Bruegel the Elder* (New York: Dover, 1963), pp. 189-211.

[262]Anderson, *Drama and Imagery,* Pl. 4a.

[263]Katzenellenbogen, *Allegories of the Virtues and Vices,* p. 73; Anderson, *The Imagery of British Churches,* p. 167.

[264]M. R. James, "The Wall Paintings in Brooke Church," in *A Supplement to Blomefield's Norfolk,* introd. Christopher Hussey (London: Clement Ingleby, 1929), Pl. V; Tristram, *English Wall Painting of the Fourteenth Century,* p. 144.

[265]See, for example, Klein, *Graphic Worlds of Peter Bruegel the Elder,* pp. 193-95.

[266]On the castle as stage property, see Merle Fifield, "The Arena Theatres in Vienna Codices 2535 and 2536," *Comparative Drama,* 2 (1968-69), 259-82, and as a symbolic building, see Roberta Cornelius, *The Figurative Castle* (Bryn Mawr, 1930); cf. F. Saxl, "A Spiritual Encyclopaedia of the Later Middle Ages," *Journal of the Courtauld and Warburg Institutes,* 5 (1942), 110-11.

[267]John Mirk, *Festial,* ed. Theodor Erbe, EETS, e.s. 96 (London, 1905), p. 203. For three further explanations of the Magdalen's name, see also Bokenham, *Legendys of Hooly Wummen,* ll. 5275ff; Bokenham indicates that he is following the account in the *Golden Legend.*

[268]T. S. R. Boase, *Castles and Churches of the Crusading Kingdom* (London: Oxford Univ. Press, 1967), p. 21.

[269]Robert H. Bowers, "The Tavern Scene in the Middle English Digby Play of Mary Magdalene," in *All These to Teach: Essays in Honor of C. A. Robertson,* ed. Robert A. Bryan et al. (Gainesville: Univ. of Florida Press, 1965), p. 15.

[270]Ibid., p. 30.

117

[271]Mirk, *Festial,* p. 203; *South English Legendary,* I, 303.

[272]*Legenda Aurea,* trans. Caxton, fol. clxxxviii.

[273]Ibid., fol. clxxxiv.

[274]Coletti, "The Design of the Digby Play of *Mary Magdalene,*" p. 319.

[275]*Jacob's Well,* p. 148. See also G. R. Owst, *Literature and Pulpit in Medieval England,* 2nd ed. (New York: Barnes and Noble, 1961), pp. 438-41.

[276]*Jacob's Well,* p. 147.

[277]Ibid., pp. 147-48.

[278]For the feast of Luxuria in illustrations of the *Psychomachia,* see the example in Helen Woodruff, *The Illustrated Manuscripts of Prudentius* (Cambridge: Harvard Univ. Press, 1930), fig. 60.

[279]James, "The Wall Paintings in Brooke Church," Pl. III; Tristram, *English Wall Painting of the Fourteenth Century,* p. 144.

[280]See especially l. 689, in which Jesus says to Mary Magdalene that "from therkness [she] hast porchasyd lyth," and see also the comments of Maltman, "Light In and On the Digby *Mary Magdalene,*" pp. 265-67.

[281]See Coletti, "The Design of the Digby Play of *Mary Magdalene,*" pp. 318-19.

[282]Louis Réau, *Iconographie de l'art Chrétien* (Paris, 1958), III, 854; A. Jameson, *Sacred and Legendary Art,* 3rd ed. (London, 1857), I, 370; Colin Slim, "Mary Magdalene, Musician and Dancer," *Early Music,* 8 (1980), 462-63.

[283]Margaret Rickert, *Painting in Britain: The Middle Ages,* 2nd ed. (Baltimore: Penguin, 1965), Pl. 38B.

[284]Richard Froning, *Frankfurter Passionspiele* (Stuttgart, 1891), pp. 403, 411-12, as cited by Slim, "Mary Magdalene, Musician and Dancer," p. 462. Sometimes, as in the Alsfeld Passion, her dancing partner is a devil; see Chauvin, "The Role of Mary Magdalene," pp. 30-31.

[285]Slim, "Mary Magdalene, Musician and Dancer," pp. 462-65. The term 'basse' would surely have involved a pun, suggesting further a kind of music condemned by such medieval writers as John of Salisbury as prostituting the voice to one's own desire; see *Frivolities of Courtiers and Footprints of Philosophers,* trans. Joseph B. Pike (Minneapolis: Univ. of Minnesota Press, 1938), pp. 33-34. For commentary on the *basse danse,* see Ingrid Brainard, "The Dance Manuals of the Late Middle Ages and Renaissance: A Survey," *EDAM Newsletter,* 6 (1984), 30-31. In an earlier play of c.1300, however, the Magdalen is said to have participated in a round dance (Slim, "Mary Magdalene, Musician and Dancer," p. 462).

[286]British Library MS. Sloan 3160, fol. 4, as quoted by A. Caiger-Smith, *English Medieval Mural Paintings* (Oxford: Clarendon Press, 1963), p. 49. Cf. Katzenellenbogen, *Allegories of the Virtues and Vices,* Pl. 66.

[287]James, "The Wall Paintings in Brooke Church," Pl. VII; Tristram, *English Wall Painting of the Fourteenth Century,* p. 144; Klein, *Graphic Worlds of Peter Bruegel,* p. 191.

[288]Chauvin, "The Role of Mary Magdalene," pp. 36-37.

[289]Etienne Houvet, *An Illustrated Monograph of Chartres Cathedral,* p. 15. See also H. W. Janson, *Apes and Ape Lore in the Middle Ages and the Renaissance* (London: Warburg Institute, 1952), pp. 112-12, 201-02; Meyer Schapiro, "On the Aesthetic Attitude in Romanesque Art," in *Romanesque Art* (New York: George Braziller, 1977), pp. 7, 25. Cf. Erwin Panofsky, *Studies in Iconology* (1939; rpt. New York: Harper, 1962), Pl. LXXVI.

[290]See Coletti, "The Design of the Digby Play of *Mary Magdalene,*" p. 327.

[291]B. Jeffery, *Chanson Verse of the Early Renaissance* (London, 1971), I, 59-60; translated by Slim, "Mary Magdalene, Musician and Dancer," pp. 59-60.

[292]Warner, *Queen Mary's Psalter,* Pl. 295a.

[293]Coletti, "The Design of the Digby Play of *Mary Magdalene,*" pp. 325-31. On Mary's change of clothing, see also especially Chauvin, "The Role of Mary Magdalene," pp. 60-61.

[294]Malvern, *Venus in Sackcloth,* fig. 9.

[295]The legend of the oil of mercy is associated with the story of the true cross, and appears to have its origin in the Gospel of Nicodemus; see *The Apocryphal New Testament,* trans. M. R. James (Oxford: Clarendon Press, 1924), pp. 126-28; see also F. E. Halliday, *The Legend of the Rood* (London: Duckworth, 1955), pp. 43-49. For the iconography related to the well of mercy, see Evelyn Underhill, "*The Fountain of Life*: An Iconographical Study," *Burlington Magazine,* 99 (1910), 99-109.

[296]See especially the discussion in Sixten Ringbom, "Devotional Images and Imaginative Devotions," *Gazette des Beaux-Arts,* 111 (1969), 159-70.

[297]On the source in early apocryphal writings of the ointment jar or box which Mary Magdalene traditionally carries, see especially Garth, *Saint Mary Magdalene in Mediaeval Literature,* pp. 33-34.

[298]R. van Luttervelt, *Masterpieces from the Great Dutch Museums* (New York: Abrams, 1961), p. 101; cf. Jameson, *Sacred and Legendary Art,* I, 371-72.

[299]See Lewis Wager, *A New Enterlude . . . entreating of the Life and Repentaunce of Marie Magdalene* (London, 1567), sigs. C3^v-C4^r, where her hair is described as "yelow as any gold. . . ." This play, which is not based on medieval legend though it utilizes techniques from the medieval theater, is discussed by Malvern, *Venus in Sackcloth,* pp. 128-35, and by Peter Happé in his chapter on the saint play in the Reformation in this book, below, pp. 226-35.

[300]Warner, *Queen Mary's Psalter,* Pl. 295b.

[301]*Legenda Aurea,* trans. Caxton, fol. clxxxiii; see also Bokenham, *Legendys of Hooly Wummen,* ll. 5274-77.

[302]Maltman, "Light In and On the Digby *Mary Magdalene,*" pp. 265-66; for Middle English translations of this hymn, see Rossell Hope Robbins, "Middle English Versions of 'Criste qui lux es et dies'," *Harvard Theological Review,* 47 (1954), 55-63. The Latin text of the hymn is conveniently reprinted from F. J. Mone, *Hymni Latini Medii Aevi,* I, 92, by Baker et al. in their edition of the Digby plays, p. 207.

[303]For a discussion of the iconography of the Lazarus plays of the Middle Ages, see Clifford Davidson, "The Visual Arts and Drama, with Special Emphasis on the Lazarus Plays," in *Le Théâtre au moyen âge,* ed. Gari Muller (Montreal: Éditions Univers, 1981), pp. 45-59.

[304]Lucy Freeman Sandler, *The Peterborough Psalter in Brussels and Other Fenland Manuscripts* (London: Harvey Miller, 1974), fig. 55.

[305]Ibid., fig. 108.

[306]Warner, *Queen Mary's Psalter,* Pl. 295c.

[307]See the description of boss 292 in the archives of the National Monuments Record, London.

[308]Christopher Woodforde, *The Norwich School of Glass-Painting in the Fifteenth Century* (London: Oxford Univ. Press, 1950), p. 49.

[309]Aina Trotzig, "Kristus som örtagårdsmästare—den nye Adam," *Iconographisk Post,* 1982/1, fig. 8.

[310]Tristram, "The Cloister Bosses of Norwich Cathedral," p. 7. A second moment shown in another boss (fig. 13), however, illustrates Christ in grave clothing as he stands with his vexillum before Mary Magdalene, who holds her long hair with one of her hands as she kneels (ibid., p. 7).

[311]W. L. Hildburgh, "English Alabaster Carvings as Records of the Medieval Religious Drama," *Archaeologia,* 93 (1949), Pl. XXI; Cheetham, *English Medieval Alabasters,* p. 284; Anderson, *Drama and Imagery,* Pl. 7a.

[312]For Adam digging with a spade in painted glass of the fifteenth century formerly at Martham, Norfolk (now at the Church of Mary Magdalene, Mulbarton), see Woodforde, *The Norwich School,* p. 169, and John Baker, *English Stained Glass* (London: Thames and Hudson, 1978), Pl. 62. The spade as a theatrical prop is treated by Steven May, "A Medieval Stage Property: The Spade," *Medieval English Theatre,* 4 (1982), 77-83.

[313]Trotzig, "Kristus som örtagårdsmästare," pp. 23-31; Garth, *Saint Mary Magdalene in Mediaeval Literature*, pp. 79-80.

[314]Ibid., p. 88.

[315]Sermo II, Migne, *PL,* CXXXIII, 720, as quoted in translation by Garth, *Saint Mary Magdalene in Mediaeval Literature*, p. 87.

[316]See May, "A Medieval Stage Property," pp. 77-78.

[317]Katzenellenbogen, *Allegories of the Virtues and Vices*, p. 75.

[318]Bede, *In Lucam Evangelium Expositio*, III; Migne, *PL,* XCII, 425, as quoted in translation by Garth, *Saint Mary Magdalene in Mediaeval Literature*, p. 83.

[319]Nigel Morgan, *Early Gothic Manuscripts [I] 1190-1250* (London: Harvey Miller, 1982), No. 30.

[320]See, for example, Bokenham, *Legendys of Hooly Wummen*, ll. 5756ff.

[321] *South English Legendary*, I, 305-06; see also Grantley, "The Source of the Digby *Mary Magdalen*," pp. 458-59.

[322]J. H. Emminghaus, *Mary Magdalene*, trans. Hans H. Rosenwald, The Saints in Legend and Art, 5 (Recklinghausen: Aurel Bongers, 1964), pp. 20-21. For further examples of the story of the Magdalen in Provence, see Réau, *Iconographie*, III, 854-55.

[323]See Katzenellenbogen, *Allegories of the Virtues and Vices*, Pls. XLIV-XLV.

[324]The immediate source for the legend is the *Golden Legend*, though the story of Mary Magdalene's final years as a hermitess appears to be strongly influenced from Anglo-Saxon times by the legend of Mary of Egypt; cf. Jean Mishrahi, "A *Vita Sanctae Mariae Magdalenae* (B.H.L. 5456) in an Eleventh-Century Manuscript," *Speculum*, 18 (1943), 335-39, and Cross, "Mary Magdalen in the *Old English Martyrology*," pp. 16-20.

[325]See Réau, *Iconographie*, III, 855-56.

[326]Pächt and Alexander, *Illuminated Manuscripts in the Bodleian Library, Oxford: 3*, No. 1312. The manuscript is said to be Flemish in origin.

[327]Glynne Wickham, *Early English Stages* (London: Routledge and Kegan Paul, 1959), I, 91 and passim, fig. 16.

[328]See Louis L. Martz, *The Poetry of Meditation*, revised ed. (New Haven: Yale Univ. Press, 1962), p. 1. Martz reproduces the painting *La Madeleine au Miroir* by Georges de la Tour of Lorraine (Collection André Fabius, Paris) on p. xxvi.

[329]Garth, *Saint Mary Magdalene in Mediaeval Literature*, pp. 85-87.

[330]St. Bernard of Clairvaux, *The Twelve Degrees of Humility and Pride*, trans. Barton R. V. Mills (London, 1929), pp. 10-11, as quoted in Martz, *The Poetry of Meditation*, p. 118.

[331]*Legenda Aurea*, trans. Caxton, fol. clxxxvii.

[332]Ibid., fol. clxxxvii.

[333]Maltman, "Light In and On the Digby *Mary Magdalene*," p. 273. *Assumpta est Maria in nubibus* is also used in the N-town *Assumption*; see JoAnna Dutka, *Music in the English Mystery Plays*, Early Drama, Art, and Music, Reference Ser., 2 (Kalamazoo: Medieval Institute Publications, 1980), p. 20.

[334]Warner, *Queen Mary's Psalter*, Pl. 296a.

[335]Ibid., Pl. 296c.

[336]Garth, *Saint Mary Magdalene in Medieval Literature*, pp. 83-85.

[337]See Mirk, *Festial*, p. 208.

[338]Szövérffy, " 'Peccatrix quonam femina'," p. 136. The association of the Magdalene with light, especially reflected light, should not be surprising, as Maltman has shown; see also the extensive background of Mary Magdalene described in Malvern, *Venus in Sackcloth*, passim.

[339]Baker et al., *The Late Medieval Religious Plays*, pp. xv-xvi; see also *The Digby Plays: Facsimiles*, fols. 38-50.

120

[340]Cf. Baker et al., *The Late Medieval Religious Plays,* pp. xix-xxi.

[341]Coldewey, "The Digby Plays and the Chelmsford Records," pp. 103-21.

[342]Arnold-Forster, *Studies in Church Dedications,* III, 12, 22, 355-58, 434-36.

[343]*Breviarium . . . ad usum insignis ecclesie Sarum* (1531), sig. ziii^v.

[344]See especially Mary del Villar, "The Staging of *The Conversion of Saint Paul,*" *Theatre Notebook,* 25 (1970-71), 64-68; Raymond Pentzell, "The Medieval Theatre in the Streets," *Theatre Survey,* 14 (1973), 1-21; Nagler, *Medieval Religious Stage,* pp. 64-67; Wickham, "The Staging of Saint Plays in England," pp. 99-119; cf. the summary of the arguments and other commentary in Baker et al., *The Late Medieval Religious Plays,* pp. xxv-xxx.

[345]Pentzell, "The Medieval Theatre in the Streets," passim.

[346]Machyn, *Diary,* p. 119.

[347]Del Villar, "The Staging of *The Conversion of Saint Paul,*" p. 67.

[348]Warner, *Queen Mary's Psalter,* Pls. 244a, 297.

[349]Claude Schaefer, *Hours of Etienne Chevalier,* trans. Marianne Sinclair (New York: George Braziller, 1971), Pl. 32; see also Jameson, *Sacred and Legendary Art,* I, 215.

[350]Tristram, "The Cloister Bosses of Norwich Cathedral," p. 15.

[351]Tristram, *English Wall Painting of the Fourteenth Century,* Pl. 53b.

[352]David E. O'Connor and Jeremy Haselock, "The Stained and Painted Glass," in *A History of York Minster,* ed. G. E. Aylmer and Reginald Cant (Oxford: Clarendon Press, 1977), Pl. 97. The source of this description of St. Paul is to be found in the apocryphal *Acts of Paul and Thecla*; see James, *The Apocryphal New Testament,* p. 273.

[353]John Capgrave, *Ye Solace of Pilgrimes: A Descripton of Rome, circa A.D. 1450,* ed. C. A. Mills and H. M. Bannister (London: Oxford Univ. Press, 1911), p. 73.

[354]Réau, *Iconographie,* III, Pt. 3, 1041. See also the Introduction, above, for comments on the iconography associated with the Fleury *Conversion of St. Paul.*

[355]Ibid., III, Pt. 3, 1042-43.

[356]Contrast the *South English Legendary*'s account of Saul's reaction (I, 265).

[357]James Torre, *The Antiquities of York Minster,* York Minster Library MS., p. 51; quoted in Davidson and O'Connor, *York Art,* p. 132.

[358]Warner, *Queen Mary's Psalter,* Pl. 244b.

[359]Compare the miniature in the English Carmelite Missal, in which Saul wears a red gown under a blue mantle. He also has blue hose. In this illustration, his attendants also have civilian clothing. See Margaret Rickert, *The Reconstructed Carmelite Missal* (Chicago: Univ. of Chicago Press, 1952), pp. 102-03, Pl. 8.

[360]*Legenda Aurea,* trans. Caxton, fol. clxxiii.

[361]See the woodcut in ibid., fol. clxxi.

[362]See Réau, *Iconographie,* III, Pt. 3, 1043.

[363]Warner, *Queen Mary's Psalter,* Pl. 301. Cf. H. S. Kingsford, *Illustrations of the Occasional Offices of the Church in the Middle Ages from Contemporary Sources,* Alcuin Club Collections, 24 (London: Mowbray, 1921), pp. 17-18, fig. 8, illustrating the baptism of Rollo the Northman.

[364]Gibson, "The Stained and Painted Glass of York," Pl. 18A.

[365]*York Plays,* ed. Beadle, Play XLIII.96sd, 109-16.

[366]On the likelihood of an East Anglian provenance for the N-town plays, see Gail McMurray Gibson, "Bury St. Edmunds, Lydgate, and the *N-Town Cycle,*" *Speculum,* 56 (1981), 56-90.

[367]*Ludus Coventriae, or The Plaie called Corpus Christi,* ed. K. S. Block, EETS, e.s. 120 (1922), pp. 352-54.

[368]*The Staging of Religious Drama,* ed. Meredith and Tailby, p. 148.

[369]*Legenda Aurea,* trans. Caxton, fol. clxxiii.

[370]See Pächt and Alexander, *Illuminated Manuscripts in the Bodleian Library, Oxford, 3,* No. 130; Morgan, *Early Gothic Manuscripts [I], 1190-1250,* Nos. 62-63, 65-66, 70, 75; Warner, *Queen Mary's Psalter,* Pl. 302.

[371]Davidson and O'Connor, *York Art,* p. 132.

[372]Tristram, *English Wall Painting of the Fourteenth Century,* p. 187; see also Caiger-Smith, *English Medieval Mural Paintings,* p. 173, for the wall painting at Hessett, Suffolk, and the fifteenth-century example at Kingston, Cambridgeshire, described as now "Obscure." See also Katzenellenbogen, *Allegories of the Virtues and Vices,* pp. 65-66.

[373]For an example in English art, see Pächt and Alexander, *Illuminated Manuscripts in the Bodleian Library, Oxford, 3,* No. 130, Pl. XII.

[374]Arnold Williams, *The Drama of Medieval England* (East Lansing: Michigan State Univ. Press, 1961), p. 164. See also the comments of Peter Happé in his review of a performance of the *Conversion of St. Paul,* at Winchester Cathedral in 1982, in *Research Opportunities in Renaissance Drama,* 25 (1982), 146.

The Saint Play in Medieval France

Lynette R. Muir

I

Drama and the Cult of Saints. Three kinds of plays make up the enormous surviving corpus of medieval French religious drama: biblical plays, saint plays, and moralities. Many individual texts, especially the early miracle plays, have been extensively and critically considered, but the saint play has not been studied as a genre, being usually lumped in together with the biblical plays as "religious" while the moralities, whether serious or comic, are generally discussed with the so-called profane or secular genres of the farce and the *sottie*.[1] The present study is an attempt to remedy this imbalance and to give some idea of the range, variety, and special qualities of the saint plays which combine the historical and didactic elements of the biblical drama with the contemporary reality and even the satirical comedy of the secular theater.

If we set aside the Anglo-Norman plays of *Adam* and the *Seinte Resurreccion*,[2] the earliest extant surviving play from France is a saint play of the kind which may be classified as a posthumous miracle play: an already dead and canonized saint intervenes in everyday life at the intercession of a devotee; this relationship of the divine and the contemporary is peculiar to these plays. Biblical drama, whether of the Old or the New Testament, is by definition historical. Even though the writers use contemporary details of clothing, manners, and way of life to emphasize the continuing reality of the Incarnation, they cannot associate the events

123

of, for example, Holy Week with the physical and tangible reality of the audience's home town in the way that can be achieved through the references to local buildings, relics, statues, and iconography in a saint play. The only true "relic" of Christ is the Eucharist (a point emphasized by the author of the *Passion de Semur*),[3] and it is thus not surprising to find a play of the miracle of the Sacrament, *La Sainte Hostie,* among the surviving sixteenth-century miracle plays.[4]

More than a hundred saint plays, counting all the miracles of Our Lady, have survived from medieval France (see the Appendix to this paper), and a considerable number of others are mentioned among the scores of recorded performances. But this is only the tip of the iceberg, for in addition to these mainly civic saint plays we know that many guilds performed the lives of their patron saints and that this drama is largely unrecorded; nor have we more than the scantiest information of the productions staged by the Confrérie de la Passion in Paris during the century and a half of regular performances before the ban of 1548 virtually put an end to religious plays being performed publicly in Paris, though in the rest of France such theatrical activity continued unabated, sometimes until the Revolution.

Stage plays were not, of course, the only manifestations of the cult of saints in the later Middle Ages; the physical reality of pilgrimage, relics, and shrines was united to the literary forms, including a huge number of verse and prose narrative lives in French and a very considerable quantity of vernacular prayers, some to individual saints for particular purposes and some in the form of general invocations and litanies. One of the most interesting of these last is the so-called *Grandes Heures,* printed by Antoine Verard in 1488, which consists of ninety-four stanzas of varying length and meter (742 lines) which, following the liturgical calendar from Circumcision (1 January) to St. Sylvester (31 December), includes all the major and many of the more popular minor saints with an indication of the particular aid for which each may be invoked. Thus in stanza 37 in July are invoked:

Amy de Dieu, glorieux saint Martin,   (4 July)
que de Cande translaté fus a Tours,
preserve moy tant au soir qu'au matin,
que les fievres n'ayent en moy le cours.
A saint Thomas le martir je recours   (7 July;
le supliant que de tentacion   translation of
me preserve par sa translation.   St. Tho. Becket)
       (ll. 282-88)

(Glorious St. Martin, friend of God, who was translated to
Tours from Candes [near Chinon], preserve me both morning
and evening that fevers may not attack me. I appeal to St.
Thomas the martyr, begging him that by his Translation he
may preserve me from temptation.)[5]

To the men and women of the fifteenth-century cities and
villages, God, like the King, was a powerful, awe-inspiring,
and somewhat remote figure. Local saints, like local over-
lords, were more accessible, among them especially the Virgin Mary and the founder-patrons of town and guild. In war-
torn and plague-ridden France, few people could travel to
Jerusalem or Rome, so local shrines and local saints attracted vast numbers of pilgrims for whom the shortness of
the spatial distance and the physical immanence of the relics
more than compensated for the temporal gap which separated them from the confessors and martyrs of the early
Church.

It is in the context of this close contact between citizen
and saint that the hagiographic drama flourished. The mass
of material makes any attempt to consider all the plays in
detail within the scope of the present study impossible, but
I have tried to give some idea of sections and groups, regional
or temporal, especially the lesser known saints of France.
Shortage of space has also meant that no reference is made
to the Passion plays, though it must not be forgotten that
they were being performed at the same time and in many of
the same communities throughout the period studied. If we
look at the performance records of some of the most dramatically active towns, we find a mixture of biblical and saint
plays though in very varying proportions: Rouen and Amiens

staged mainly biblical plays, while Compiègne and Laval had mainly saint plays, and Metz with the most recorded productions outside of Paris staged the Passion only once between 1409 and 1520 against fourteen different miracle and saint plays.[6]

If we extend this survey to other European countries, we find equally wide and inexplicable variations, not all of which can be attributed to the random chance of survival of text or record. While no country has a bulk of material remotely comparable to the French, Spain and Italy do both possess a considerable number of short saint plays, with, in the case of the former, also a wide variety of scenes of allegorical or doctrinal significance, bearing some resemblance to the French *moralités* and dating mainly from the sixteenth century; the Peninsula is, however, very short on straightforward Passion plays.[7] Italy, on the other hand, has a very large number of short plays on episodes from both Old and New Testaments as well as lives and miracles of the post-biblical saints. Nor did the Renaissance cult of classical antiquity prevent many of these religious plays from being printed in the fifteenth and sixteenth centuries.[8] In Northern Europe, the situation is very different. England has three extant saint plays and a number of records of performances, while Germany has a bare handful of saint plays (most of them being miracles rather than hagiographic plays), yet including three versions of the Theophilus legend and three plays of the Invention of the Holy Cross.[9] Both England and Germany had, of course, biblical plays, and in the latter the saints were extensive and important, surviving in the Catholic areas through the sixteenth and into the seventeenth century at Lucerne, for example, while the Oberammergau and some of the Tyrolean plays have persisted to the present time.[10]

Comparative studies of these varied traditions would be useful for both dramatic and sociological purposes, for hagiographic literature is one of the most important mirrors of medieval life, thought, and popular religion, and its dramatic manifestations in particular are a treasure trove of social, cultural, and literary reflections.[11]

II

Miracle plays: St. James and St. Nicholas. The vast majority of the plays in which the saint appears as *deus ex machina* relate miracles of Our Lady—more than fifty of them have survived in French—but two other saints also feature in this kind of play, St. James as the protector of pilgrims on the way to his shrine at Compostella and St. Nicholas in a variety of different incidents.

The only surviving miracle of St. James from France is the incomplete Provençal *Ludus Sancti Jacobi,*[12] a dramatization of the well-known legend of the young man who rejects a woman's advances, is wrongfully accused of theft, and is hanged while on his way to Santiago. His parents invoke St. James, and the hanged man is unharmed. The local judge is finally convinced of the innocence of the accused by the miracle of the roast chicken on his dinner table starting to crow. (This theme also occurs in English in the *Ballad of King Herod and the Cock* and in French as part of the story of Judas in *The Passion des Jongleurs.*[13]) There is, as we shall see below, a possible link between the *Ludus* and some wall paintings in the Briançon region of Dauphiné.

St. Nicholas, one of the most popular saints of medieval and modern Europe, is the only non-biblical saint to figure in liturgical Latin music-dramas, perhaps because he was the patron of scholars, among many other groups. This is at least hinted at in Wace's *Vie de Saint Nicolas* (c.1150). At the end of the narrative of the miraculous resuscitation of the three clerks murdered on their way to school, Wace explains:

> Pur ceo qu'as clercs fit cel honur
> Funt li clers la feste a son jur
> De ben lirë et ben chanter
> Et des miracles reciter. (ll. 223-26)

(Because he did the clerks this honor, the clerks celebrate his feast day by reading and singing well and reciting the miracles.)

At the beginning of the *Vie,* Wace explains his reasons for writing and his choice of French rather than Latin as the language in which to compose his *Life:*

> A ces qui n'unt lectres aprises
> Ne lur ententes n'i ont mises,
> Deivent li clerc mustrer la lei.
> Parler des seinz, dire pur quei
> Chescone feste est controvee,
> Chescone a sun jur gardee . . .
> En romanz dirrai de sa vie
> Et des miracles grant partie . . .
> Que li lai le puissent aprendre,
> Qui ne poënt latin entendre. (ll. 1-6, 39-40, 43-44)

(For those who have not learned to read nor given their attention to this, the clerks must explain the Law. [They must] talk of the saints and explain why each feast-day has been established and is kept on its day. . . . I will tell you of his life in French and a great number of the miracles so that the laity, who are unable to understand Latin, can learn about them.)[14]

Of the many miracles recounted by Wace, four were dramatized in Latin, two of them—the dowerless girls and the "pickled boys"—in both France and Germany.[15] Latin plays in which the bishop of Myra appears as a guardian of treasure are to be found in the works of Hilarius and in the Fleury Playbook, while the same story, the *Iconia,* forms the subject of the earliest and finest of all French saint plays, Jean Bodel's *Jeu de St. Nicolas,* one of the masterpieces of medieval drama.[16]

In Bodel's version of the story (which agrees with Hilarius rather than with Fleury), the soldiers of a pagan king having slaughtered the crusading Christian invaders bring back to the king as prisoner a *preud'hom* and his *mahommet cornu*—a statue of St. Nicholas in episcopal mitre (l. 458). Questioned by the king, the *preud'hom* sings the praises of the saint and mentions among other attributes that

> Il fait ravoir toutes les pertes . . .
> Riens que en se garde soit mise
> N'iert ja perdue ne maumise,
> Tant ne sera abandonnee. (ll. 521, 526-28)

128

(He brings back everything that is lost. . . . Nothing which is
put under his guard will ever be lost or damaged however
neglected it may be.)

Naturally the king must test this marvel, and the rest of
the play describes how thieves, learning that the royal treasure is guarded only by a statue, immediately steal it but are
forced to return their spoils when St. Nicholas appears in
person and threatens them. The play ends with the conversion of the king and his emirs, thus fulfilling another of the
preud'hom's claims that "Il rapele les mescreans" ("He recalls the unbeliever," 1. 523). This *Iconia* miracle is not, to
my knowledge, ever portrayed in art and the other miracle
dramatized in French, the *Miracle de St. Nicolas et d'un Juif,*
very rarely.[17] This story relates how a Jew lends a Christian
money without any guarantee except an oath sworn by St.
Nicholas. The Christian tricks the Jew but is soon after killed
by a man driving a cart—a scene depicted in a panel from
a window in York Minster[18]—and the deceit is revealed. The
Jew generously begs St. Nicholas to restore the dead man,
promising to become a Christian if this is done. The resus-
citated trickster is a reformed character, unlike the thieves
in Bodel's play who remain unrepentant rogues.

The sudden, short-lived flowering of Nicholas plays in
France at the end of the twelfth century was followed by a
period of total neglect until the sixteenth century which saw,
in addition to the play described above, a lost play of *St.
Nicolas de Bari* performed in Metz in 1513.[19] It seems likely
that the explanation of this phenomenon is the immense up-
surge of miracles of Our Lady, narrative ones in the late
twelfth and thirteenth centuries as well as dramatic examples
from the late thirteenth century through the fourteenth and
fifteenth to the middle of the sixteenth. The Nicholas miracles are limited in scope and specific in subject, and not all
are dramatically effective. In comparison, the unlimited powers of the Virgin and her role as universal mediatrix meant
that any kind of theme, story, or incident could be and was
given dramatic form as a *Miracle de la Vierge*.

III

The life and miracles of Our Lady. Mother of God and Queen of Heaven, the Virgin Mary has a major role in more plays than any other human character. In Passion plays her part was often extensively developed not only in the *planctus* or lament over the death of her Son, but also in additional scenes such as Jesus' farewell to his Mother before the Entry into Jerusalem or the appearance to her of the newly-risen Christ. In Nativity plays, however, the role is usually more closely linked with explicitly biblical material, though one play, from a convent at Huy in Belgium, includes a scene where St. Anne visits her daughter and the Christ Child, accompanied by the Virgin's sisters, Mary Jacobi and Mary Salome.[20]

In the fourteenth and fifteenth centuries, growing devotion to the Virgin and the spread of the doctrine of the Immaculate Conception (though it was not to be declared dogma until 1854) led to the composition of scenes and even whole plays on the Conception, Birth, and Childhood of Mary both in French and in Latin: the Feast of the Presentation of Mary in the Temple, introduced from the East, was celebrated in Avignon in 1372, and a dramatic form of the event to accompany the Office was composed by Philippe de Mézières. It includes detailed staging directions.[21]

The Virgin's role in plays was also extended to include the period after the Resurrection and Ascension, finally culminating in the Assumption plays which were particularly popular in Spain where the town of Elche still celebrates the Feast with a two-day performance, the Death of the Virgin on 14 August and the Assumption on the next day. In both scenes of this sung vernacular play, use is made of the *ara celi*—the machine for raising and lowering the inhabitants of heaven—which was already being used in the Middle Ages. The Assumption play is also found in France, though the Passions normally end with the Resurrection appearances, the Ascension, or (at latest) Pentecost. (The only exception is the Valenciennes twenty-day cyclic play which runs from

Creation to the Assumption.) Unlike the English cycles, therefore, the French biblical plays never include the Last Judgment: Doomsday is always treated as a separate subject and includes a substantial role for the Virgin, though it is ultimately made clear that her powers as mediatrix end at the Last Coming.[22]

Prior to the Last Judgment, however, Mary's power is virtually unlimited, a fact attested by the hundreds of stories and dozens of plays which describe her miraculous intervention on behalf of her suppliants. The earliest play on this theme, Rutebeuf's *Miracle de Théophile* (c.1270), sets the pattern with the story of the priest Théophile who sells his soul to the devil for preferment, repents, and prays to the Virgin because he dare not pray to God.[23] Our Lady rebukes him severely but accepts his repentance and forces the devil to return the charter by threatening him: "Je te foulerai la pance" ("I shall trample on your belly," l. 585). This rather crude-sounding threat is probably based on the promise in *Genesis* that the seed of the woman will triumph over the serpent: "she shall crush thy head" (3.15; *Douay-Rheims*).

Dramatic miracles of the Virgin proliferated in France and continued to be written well into the sixteenth century, but the most important collection is that found in the Cangé manuscript and normally simply referred to as the *Miracles de la Vierge*.[24] These forty short plays (none is over five thousand lines and many are half that length) were written for the goldsmiths' guild of Paris. One of the plays was performed each year between 1339 and 1382 on the occasion of the annual meeting (*siège*) of the *Confrérie Saint Eloi*, the patron of the guild.[25] The subject matter of the plays includes biblical, historical, and contemporary themes with a number of other saints being featured also, some in well-known versions of their legends and others, e.g., St. Guillem-du-désert (the epic hero Guillaume d'Orange) in a unique story—unique, that is, in French, for the archives of Lucerne contain a stage-plan for a play of St. William performed in 1596, and a comparison of the characters listed on the plan with those in the Cangé play make it clear that the two plays use substantially the same material.[26]

The Cangé miracles contain few indications of staging or iconography save that the Virgin is regularly accompanied by angels with music and lights when she appears to her votaries. However, the considerable number of plays which depict the Virgin intervening in fourteenth-century France presented many a vivid tableau of contemporary society; indeed in some cases the play is virtually a secular drama of bourgeois life with minimal divine intervention. In the *Miracle de l'enfant ressuscité*,[27] for example, there is a scene of the wife going into labor with loud cries and complaints and the maid sending the boy to fetch the midwife, who comments acidly:

> Espoir sant elle mal es rains
> Du fais de lenfant qu'elle porte,
> Si lui est avis qu'elle est morte,
> Se tantost n'a la sage femme.
> Pour ce qu'elle est bien riche dame
> Non pour quant, voulentiers iray.
> De li bien paier me feray. (ll. 416-22)

(I expect she's got a pain in the back from the weight of the child she's carrying, and thinks she'll die if the midwife doesn't come at once. Still, she's a very rich lady, I'll go willingly and make sure I'm well paid by her.)

After the birth the maid recommends the new mother to have a bath to ease her discomfort, while she herself goes next door to fetch a neighbor to cheer her up. This well-intentioned advice has disastrous consequences: drowsy from the warm water, the mother drops the child, who is drowned. She is arrested and condemned to be burned but welcomes death lest "par longue doulour/ Ne renie mon creatour" ("lest through prolonged grief I come to deny my Creator," ll. 1496-97). The husband meanwhile invokes the aid of the Virgin, and after the mother has begged to hold her dead child a final time, it is put into her arms and cries: "Icy crie l'enfant" (l. 1581). This is one of the few stage directions in the manuscript. The play ends with a general thanksgiving by all the people in church as well as rejoicing in heaven, at the end of which the Virgin suggests they visit the husband and wife who have already left the stage, thus motivating the processional exit of the heavenly party. Entrances and exits were, of course, difficult on the curtainless medieval stage.

Miracle plays usually depict the contemporary scene, whereas plays on a saint's life normally belong, like biblical plays, to what Alan Knight has described as the historical genres, though here the term 'historical' needs to be taken in its medieval sense.[28] A number of plays on the miracles of the Virgin, however, involve historical characters, either saints such as Lawrence or Alexis or secular figures such as Robert le Diable or Clovis. Conversely, some of the biographical plays depict the lives of more or less contemporary saints (give or take a century or so) such as Louis IX or Catherine of Siena, while in others there are many details of medieval life—details similar to those presented in the miracle plays. Nowhere is this mingling of the thaumaturgical and biographical elements so noticeable as in the dramatizations of the lives of the two virgin saviors of France, Genevieve and Joan.

IV

The Miracles de Sainte Geneviève and the Siège d'Orléans: Saints of France. A group of short plays on the life and miraculous works of Geneviève, patron saint of Paris, are to be found with other biblical and saint plays in the fifteenth-century manuscript, MS. 1131 in the Bibliothèque Sainte-Geneviève in Paris.[29] The plays themselves probably date from the late fourteenth century, and it has been suggested, though the idea is not susceptible of proof, that they formed the early repertory of the celebrated Confrérie de la Passion, which was given a formal charter by the king in 1402 when it had already been in existence for some years and which, after many vicissitudes, was finally to be disbanded by Louis XIV in 1668.[30]

133

Most of the saint plays in MS. 1131 are of a conventional
type, including a sequence of the Premiers Martyrs, Stephen, Peter, Paul, and Denis:

> vraiement de latin en françois
> rimé, à la gloire et honneur
> de Dieu et de ses sains
> soit et au profit de noz
> ames, etc.   (Prologue)

(translated truly and accurately from Latin into French verse,
may it be to the honor and glory of God and his saints and
the profit of our souls, etc.)[31]

The plays of St. Geneviève are very different. From the rubric which introduces the first of them—"C'est le miracle
comment les anges firent joye quant madame Ste Geneviève
fut née"—and the scene of angels singing in heaven after her
birth, it is obvious that the author intends to model his heroine and her life as far as possible on the Virgin Mary. The
second play in this roughly chronological series describes her
as *la Saincte Vierge* in the rubric, and, in a scene reminiscent
of John the Baptist's witness to the divinity of Christ, St.
Germain of Auxerre en route for England to deal with the
Pelagian heresy (*l'eresie qui mehaigne*/ *Ly pluseurs de la
Grant Bertaigne*) sees her in the crowd and says:

> Je voy là une damoiselle
> Saincte et dévote et bonne et belle
> Remplie de la grace Dieu. (p. 173)

(There I see a maiden, holy, devout, good, and beautiful,
filled with the grace of God.)

He speaks to Geneviève, confirms her in her desire to live
in virginity, and foretells that she will lead a holy life saving
many sinners by her teaching and by her merits.

After her parent's death, Geneviève goes to Paris, and
a detailed stage direction describes how the new scene is to
be set:

> Lors se tiengne devant Paris un pou avant ou champ, et il-
> lecques soit un petit autel suz le quel soit l'image Nostre-
> Dame, et devant l'autel une fourmete pour soit mettre a oroi-
> son et bien près soit son lit fait de une table en hault et un
> povre couverteur dessuz et l. oreillier de bois. (p. 181)

> (Then let her stop in front of Paris a little downstage, and
> there let there be a small altar on which is an image of Our
> Lady and in front of the altar a small bench where she can
> say her prayers, and close by let there be her bed made of a
> table for the top and a poor covering below with a wooden
> pillow.)

In the succeeding plays she sees visions, cures the sick, and by her intercessions—mediated to Our Lady by SS. Peter, Paul, John, and Denis in full canonicals—she saves Paris from destruction by the Huns (*Hondres*). In another play she prays for a child who through his mother's fault has died unbaptised. There is a vigorous scene here between St. Michael and the devils who argue that the child belongs to them by God's own law: "Ou el est fausse ou elle est bonne:/ S'el est bonne l'enfant est nostre" ("Either it [the law] is good or it is false. If it is good, the child is ours," p. 240). Similar arguments in the *Miracles de la Vierge* leave the devils equally disgruntled. In this play, Satan tries to appeal against the verdict, finally commenting rudely that "celle truande/ Genevieve a tant flajolé/ Qu'el a Dieu du tout afolé" ("This whore Geneviève has whistled so much she's got God completely confused," p. 243). A tug-of-war ensues between the angels and devils with each holding one end of the image which here, as usually in medieval drama and iconography, represents the soul. The devils are finally driven off, and Michael puts the soul by the child's body, telling Geneviève that he is alive and should be baptised at once. This play is one of the liveliest of this generally varied and entertaining sequence which deserves to be much more widely known.

A quarter of a century after the founding of the Confrérie de la Passion, a new virgin savior, Joan, Maid of Orleans, appeared in France and was commemorated in a play. Five hundred years were to elapse before her canonization so that the *Siège d'Orléans*[32] may not technically be a saint play, though there is very clear evidence that Joan of Arc was already considered a saint by her contemporaries. The full title of the play—*Le Mistère du Siège d'Orléans*—makes it clear that it was not written simply as a historical drama despite the very considerable proportion of the text which is given over to scenes of battle and war. A stage direction at line 2230 will suffice to indicate this latter aspect of the play:

> Puis ceulx d'Orleans sauldront en armes au devant et sonnera le beffroy et cryront à l'arme! D'un cousté et d'autre, canons, trompetes; et en y aura beaucoup mors d'un cousté et d'autre; et à la fin, se reculleront les François en leur boulvart fait de fagotz et de terre devant les Tourelles.

> (Then the people of Orleans will leap out in front, armed, and the bells will ring in the tower and they will cry "To arms!" Cannons and trumpets on each side; and there will be many dead on both sides; and finally the French will retire behind their bulwark made of brushwood and earth in front of the Tourelles [i.e., part of the fortifications of the town].)

In marked contrast to this scene of contemporary warfare is that based on the Debate in Heaven from the biblical plays, in which Charles, the uncrowned king of France, prays "devant paradis" ("in front of heaven," l. 6813) for God's succor for the people of France and Orleans in particular. Two saintly former bishops of the city, Evortius (Euvertre) and Anianus (Aignan), join with the Virgin Mary to intercede with God, who finally announces that while the French must be punished for their sins, the king's prayer would be answered. Then he orders St. Michael to go to the little village of Domremy:

> La trouveras, sans plus enquerre,
> Une pucelle par honneur . . .
> Tu luy diras que je luy mande
> Qu'en elle sera ma vertu
> Et que par elle on entende
> L'orgueil des François abatu. (ll. 7014, 7020-23)

> (There you will find without further inquiry a maiden most honorable. . . . You will tell her the message I send her that my power will be in her, and by her the pride of the French will be held abased.)

The similarity to the Annunciation is continued in the dialogue between Michael and Joan, who is referred to throughout the text as La Pucelle, "the Maid." Michael's opening words echo the *Ave Maria*: "Jeune pucelle bien eureuse,/ Le Dieu du ciel vers vous m'envoye" ("Young and most blessed maid, the God of Heaven sends me to you," ll. 7060-61). Joan expresses her fear and her ignorance of arms, but is finally convinced and sets out on her mission. It is notable that this play, like the *Miracles de Ste Geneviève*, does not include the death of the heroine: these are not martyrdom plays but plays of the deeds and life of the protagonist.

A considerable number of other French saint plays make use of this combination of patriotism, miracles, and edification. Some, like the play of St. Clement, bishop of Metz, or the four plays on the life of St. Martin of Tours, include the death-bed of the saint, but in these dramas the death is peaceful and edifying, visually and verbally.[33] One example that deals more with miracles is that of St. Rémy, the patron of Rheims who converted and anointed Clovis and brought France to Christianity—a play that ends with an epilogue asking God to grant peace to France.[34]

Certainly peace was a subject dear to the hearts of French audiences in the fifteenth century. It is interesting to see the changing stress in the two plays on the life of St. Louis, one written in the fifteenth and one in the sixteenth century. The former, a three-day play, develops the conflict between the saintly king and the English, who are portrayed speaking what can only be called franglais! In Gringore's *St. Louis,* composed about 1512, however, there is much greater emphasis on the clash between Louis and the emperor Frederic over the latter's persecution of the Church.[35]

A different form of contemporary influence in these plays of the Confessors and Doctors of the church is that seen in the play on the life of St. Dominic and the *Institution de l'ordre des Freres Prescheurs,*[36] which lays stress on the corruption and heresy in France, or in the *Mystère de Saint Bernard de Menthon,* which describes the establishment of the famous hospice on the Great-St-Bernard Pass and refers to the benefits this foundation has brought to the pilgrims who pass this way to Rome.[37]

The plays discussed in this section all deal with the Church and the development of Christianity through the activities of the saints concerned. Despite the scenes of warfare and battle, they are not primarily violent plays: like the miracles, they are mainly concerned with living, not dying— with salvation rather than martyrdom. The next group of plays to be considered will more than rectify this imbalance.

V

Saints of the New Testament and the Early Church: (a) The glorious company of the Apostles. In addition to the Virgin Mary, who has been considered separately, all the apostles and several other New Testament figures (e.g., Mary Magdalene and Stephen the proto-martyr) were made the subject of plays in the fifteenth century. It is worth noting that in France St. Denis is always included with this group although he is not strictly scriptural. As early as the ninth century the Apostle of Gaul became conflated with Denis or Dionysius the Areopagite, the Neoplatonist converted to Christianity by St. Paul in Athens. According to the *Golden Legend,* Denis saw the eclipse which occurred at the time of the death of Christ—an eclipse which was visible in Greece and Egypt as well as in Palestine—and declared that it signified the coming of the true light which would bring light to the world.[38] The patron saint of France thus joins the select company of the twelve, and in addition to an incomplete play on his life he is included in the *Ste-Geneviève* sequence of the *Premiers Martyrs*[39] as well as in the very long, wideranging, and popular *Actes des Apôtres,* attributed to the Greban brothers, which survived in two manuscripts and several printed editions, one of them giving the text of the 1536 production of the play in Bourges. There are many details extant of this performance whose costumes were of unparalleled richness while the *feintes* or special effects run to many pages in the printed list.[40]

138

In addition to the two groups of the *Ste-Geneviève* and the Greban plays, a number of other texts have survived from different parts of France which describe the deeds, miracles, and death of the apostles, especially SS. Peter and Paul who are normally treated together.[41] Apart from the Greban texts, however, these Apostle plays seem to have offered little scope for developing the scenes of torture and violence that characterize the very popular dramatizations of the martyrdom of the victims of the early persecutions of the Church in which a good torture scene, on stage, sweetened many a lengthy sermon for the medieval spectator.

(b) The noble army of martyrs. Some of the best known and most popular saints of medieval Europe had suffered martyrdom and were honored in play and picture in many different countries. Among the women, the most renowned were St. Catherine of Alexandria and (in France) St. Barbe or Barbara.[42] Of the men, SS. Crispin and Crispinian, patron saints of shoemakers, were popular in France and Spain;[43] St. Lawrence, whose gridiron was depicted on many a church wall or woodwork, shares a play with St. Hippolitus (*La vie de monseigheur sainct Laurens par personnaiges. Avec le martire de sainct Ypolite*),[44] who was dramatically martyred by being torn apart by horses. St. George, most notable for his defeat of the dragon in later art and literature and treated below in this chapter, was also a widely revered martyr whose sufferings were staged in France, Italy, and Spain. A common feature of the French martyrdom plays is a staging prologue describing the multiple locations such as is found in the St. Crispin, St. Lawrence, and St. Vincent plays and in the shorter of the two versions of the life of St. Barbe, that in two days, which was reprinted several times in the sixteenth century—a clear testament to its popularity.[45]

Another feature of both Martyrdom and Confessor plays is the emphasis on the miracles wrought by the relics of the saints and also often the representation of the translation of these relics. It is obvious from the comments in the epilogues to some of these texts that the performance was particularly

139

designed to attract pilgrims to the shrines—e.g., the end of the *St. Margaret* play when *Colombe* (the Dove) comes down from heaven and addresses the much tortured Margaret immediately before she is beheaded.[46]

> *Pause. Adonc Colombe descend de Paradis et vient a Marguerite.*
>
> > . . . Moy qui suis colombe sans fiel
> > Je t'annonce que tous tes serfs
> > Ne seront en nul temps desers
> > En paix seront et pacifiques
> > Et en tous lieux ou tes relicques
> > Seront posees ou ta vie
> > Dieu ne les oubliera mye.[47]

> (*Pause. Then Dove comes down from Paradise to Margaret.* I, who am dove without bitterness, announce to you that all your followers will never at any time be deserted. They will live in peace, tranquilly. And any place where your relics or your *Vita* are kept will not be forgotten by God.)

VI

French saint or foreign saint? Reasons for the choice of play. A consideration of the lists of performances drawn up by Petit de Julleville and complemented by the subsequent work of other scholars raises almost more problems than it solves. In a few cases, such as the play of St. Didier at Lengres or of St. Quentin in the town of that name, the element of local patriotism would seem to provide a clear reason for the choice. Indeed, Guillaume Flamand, the author of the St. Didier play, expressly states that he has written it "à la requeste de messieurs les confrères de la confrarie dud. sainct aud. Lengres" ("at the request of the honorable brothers of the brotherhood of the said saint in the said Lengres"[48]) and adds that it was performed by them in 1482. However, Flamand was not the first person to dramatize the life of this little-known saint, who had been honored with a dramatic performance in Montélimar thirty years before, as we know from a council minute of 25 April 1448 referring to the preparation of the *Place La Pierre* where the *jeu de saint Didier* was to be performed.[49]

140

An alternative to local connections is afforded by guild patronage. The masons and carpenters of Paris commissioned the play of their patron, St. Louis, from Pierre Gringore, while the *Mystère de Sainte Venice* (better known as Veronica) was performed for a *confrarie* which invoked also St. Fiacre. The only guild to venerate this unlikely pair of saints was that of the Master Gardeners in Paris.[50] But sometimes a play was produced not for a trade guild but rather for a religious confraternity such as the Confrérie de Saint Jacques-aux-pelerins.[51] In certain cases, both kinds of groups were instrumental in arranging the performance, as in the case of the play of *SS. Crispin and Crispinian* on their feast day (14 May) in Paris in 1458: the manuscript tells us that it was the property of the "confrarie monseigneur saint Crespin et monseigneur saint Crespinien fondée en l'église Notre Dame de Paris aux maistres et aux compaignons cordouenniers."[52] The cordwainers or shoemakers guild may perhaps have lent their text for the performance at Compiègne in 1488, though this can only be speculation.[53] What is certain is that although the relics of the saints were preserved at Soissons, not far from Paris, there is no record of a performance in that town. Nor did St. Martin apparently ever get a performance of his life in his native Tours, though the records for the Loire area are so incomplete that such an assertion cannot be definitive, but he was sufficiently popular in other parts of France to have four plays which survive— more than for any other saint of the post-biblical period.[54]

Relics, guild and confraternity patronage, pilgrimage, and local patriotism do not exhaust the reasons for the choice of play. Another of considerable significance is the saint's ability to preserve a community against pestilence and plague. St. George was among the group noted for this all over Europe, and hence many leper houses were placed under his nominal protection. Almost as effective were the efforts of St. Sebastian, and four performances of plays on this saint are recorded between 1546 and 1567 in the Maurienne area of Savoy. The first, in Beaune, was explicitly the result of a vow made "pour obvier et preserver les manants et habitants du dict Beaune d'icelle infection de peste" ("to defend and preserve the dwellers and inhabitants in Beaune from this pestilential affliction").[55]

Relics of St. Sebastian had been taken to France in the ninth century to the church of St. Médard at Soissons, while relics were also venerated at St. Victor in Paris: during the Black Death they were carried in procession in the city. It has been suggested that the traditional iconography of the saint, with his body pierced by numerous arrows, accounts for the particular invocation of Sebastian against the plague,[56] but this would not account for the other saints who were also invoked in this extremity—e.g., St. Roch or St. Adrien, whose relics at Grammont in Flanders were linked with a strong local cult of this Byzantine saint. The play of the latter saint's life and martyrdom also comes from the northern French/Flemish region.[57]

A solitary example of individual patronage of a personal patron saint is that recorded from Metz where in 1468 Dame Catherine Baudoiche had performed at her expense a play of St. Catherine of Siena, who had been canonized only seven years earlier. Among the notable details of this play is the fact that the role of Catherine was taken by a young girl. This is the earliest but by no means the only example of women performing in mystery plays in France.[58] It seems possible that the nature of the life of Catherine of Siena, with her role as intermediary between warring popes and princes, her life of ascetic simplicity, and her death in the odor of sanctity, made the choice of a girl less surprising than it would have been in, for example, a martyrdom play.

Whatever the play and whatever the reason for the choice in different parts of France, no area is so well documented or so interesting as the southeastern provinces of Dauphiné and Savoy.

VII

The saint play in Savoy and Dauphiné: Examples of regional drama. In the early sixteenth century, the regions of

France on the borders with Italy and Provence were exceptionally rich in religious drama, especially saint plays. Some of the many surviving texts portray little-known local saints, as in the example of the celebrated play of the *Trois Doms* from Romans in 1509 which has survived complete with accounts and performance-details of all kinds.[59] The *text* of this play, like the names of the three "lords"—Félicien, Exupère, and Séverin—is virtually unknown and unstudied. It is not without originality, however, not least in being the only known play in which *all* the women's roles were played by women—including the unusual allegorical figures who open the play. In this prologue, Dame Silance announces a forthcoming *mystère,* and then "come the three corners of the world" as each continent, from a tower at one corner of the rectangular central stage, boasts in turn of her might and power. Asia claims the pre-eminence as the acknowledged paragon of excellence (l. 33) but is brusquely interrupted by Africa, who insists she has superseded Asia as "sovereign princess of the regions" (l. 37). She in turn is rejected as inferior by Europe, sustained by all Christians, the truly happy knights (l. 50). When Silance, the precise significance of whose name is never made clear, questions the continents, all three declare their intention of attending the *mystère.* Silance tells Africa and Asia it is not for them as pagans and infidels who do not believe in the Virgin Mary, but she promises to join Europe in her tower to hear the play; then she admonishes the spectators to listen in silence and to prepare for the appearance of the Romans who are violently opposed to the faith of Christ. At this point she gives the signal to begin: "You will make your entrance when ready, Sir Severus, *grant empereur romain*" (l. 114).

The characters of this prologue do not remain permanently on view in the tower watching the play, as we can tell from the fact that all of the actresses later play other roles. Europe, played by Louise, daughter of Jean de Manicieu, was also the Emperor of Rome's daughter, while Claude changed from the dignified Dame Silance into *Poudrefine,* the torturers' tart. Africa and Asia later played *Inspiration Divine* and *Grace Divine*.

Neither are the towers wasted, for at the opening of the second day they feature as watchtowers manned by the *tirans* armed with arbalests and couleuvrines. The play itself is conventional in structure, alternating scenes of war and torture with exhortations by the saints who are encouraged not by angels but by attributes of God such as *Comfort Divin*. An interesting variation on the Palm Sunday tradition of casting down branches before Christ on his donkey is provided by the scene in which the citizens of the town cast thorns and thistles in the path of the saints as they are dragged along amid a torrent of stones and abuse towards the place of martyrdom. Other good visual effects are the descent of *Comfort Divin,* who "s'avancera sur sa fainte" during a "pose d'orghes" (l. 8967). It is not clear how this *feinte* was worked, but a rope and pulley structure seems most likely. A similar kind of machine is needed in the torture scene when the tyrants, helped by *Poudrefine,* prepare a primitive guillotine or *moton,* carefully adjusting it so that the blade only cuts part way through Séverin's neck. When he has finished his prayer he takes his place under the *moton* and the trapdoor turns, leaving a dummy, a *corps feint,* to be beheaded.

Although the Romans play is one of the longest and most widely known of the Dauphiné saint plays, it is far from being the only one. Chocheyras, in his two great studies of the drama in the regions of Savoy and Dauphiné through to the eighteenth century, has made it quite clear that certain districts in each of these provinces had a flourishing and local dramatic tradition often over two or three centuries. In contrast to the long civic plays of the Bas-Dauphiné represented by the Romans play, there is in that province a group of much shorter plays, in Provençal, from the Briançon region in the mountainous southeast corner of the province, including texts of *SS. Peter and Paul, St. Eustache,* and *St. Anthony,* the Desert Father famous for the Temptation to which he was subjected.[60] The editor of this last play explains that relics of the saint were brought to Dauphiné in 1076 by a certain

INDEX

INDEX

INDEX

1. The Jew praying to St. Nicholas. Sketch from painted glass (now too corroded to photograph), St. Severus Chapel, Rouen Cathedral.

2. St. Denys. Painted glass, Church of St. Denys, York. Copyright: David E. O'Connor by kind permission of the vicar, the Rev. T. Preston.

3. The Martyrdom of St. Denys and St. Denys carrying his head before a church. Cloister boss, Norwich Cathedral. Copyright: Royal Commission on the Historical Monuments of England.

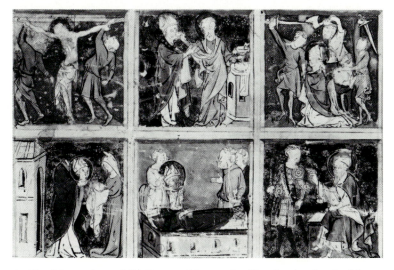

4. The Martyrdom of St. Denys. Manuscript illumination by the Master of the Queen Mary Psalter. Bodleian Library MS. Canon Misc. 248, fol. 45ᵛ (detail). By courtesy of the Curators of the Bodleian Library, Oxford.

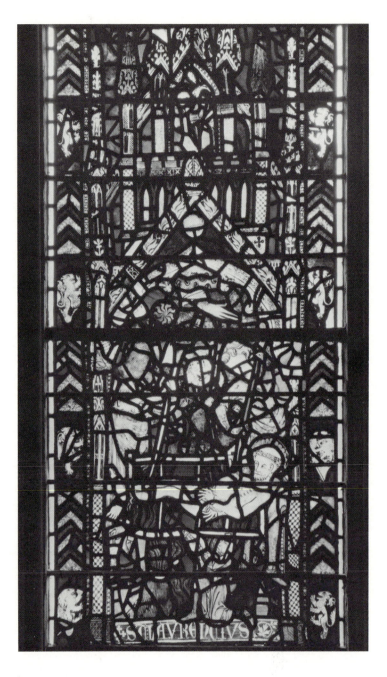

5. The Martyrdom of St. Lawrence. Painted glass, York Minster nave.
Copyright: Royal Commission on the Historical Monuments of England.

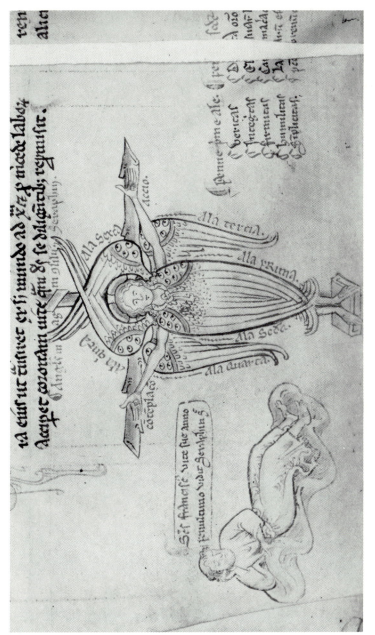

6. Seraph appearing to St. Francis. Manuscript illumination by Matthew Paris. Corpus Christi College MS. 16, fol. 66ᵛ. By permission of the Master and Fellows of Corpus Christi College, Cambridge.

7. Life of St. Catherine. Wall Painting, Sporle, Norfolk. Copyright: Royal Commission on the Historical Monuments of England.

8. St. Catherine refuses to worship an idol. Alabaster. British Museum. Courtesy of the Trustees of the British Museum.

9. The Martyrdom of St. Thomas Becket. Alabaster. British Museum.
Courtesy of the Trustees of the British Museum.

10. St. George receives armor from the Blessed Virgin Mary. Restored painted glass, St. Neot, Cornwall. Copyright: Royal Commission on the Historical Monuments of England.

11. St. Mary Magdalene. Painted screen (detail), Wiggenhall. Copyright: Royal Commission on the Historical Monuments of England.

12. Lucas van Leyden, *The Worldly Pleasures of Mary Magdalene*. Engraving.

14. Mary Magdalene. Detail from painted glass, East Harling, Norfolk. Copyright: Royal Commission on the Historical Monuments of England.

13. Hortulanus scene, with Mary Magdalene and Risen Christ. Roof boss, nave, Norwich Cathedral. Copyright: Royal Commission on the Historical Monuments of England.

15. St. Barbe defeats the pagan doctors in argument. Painted roof, Church of St Martin-des-Connées.

16. St. Barbe defies her Mother, the Queen. Painted roof, Church of St
Martin-des-Connées.

17. St. George triumphs over the magician Athanaise whose poisoned cup has killed the man at saint's feet though the saint himself is unharmed. Woodcarving, choir stalls, St. George's Chapel, Windsor Castle. By permission of the Dean and Chapter.

18. St. Herculaneum holding an image with structures around the Great Square in Perugia, structures now altered or destroyed. Painted by Meo di Guido or his collaborator. National Gallery, Perugia. Copyright: Fot. Alinari.

19. Beheading of St. John the Baptist. Painted by Giannicola di Paolo, 1515. Chapel of St. John the Baptist, Collegio del Cambio, Perugia. Copyright: Fot. Alinari.